BEYOND BABEL

An Understanding of the
Timeless Universal Principles
Required to Build Excellent Organizations

Gerald R. Chester, Ph.D.

Excel Digital Press • Dallas, Texas

Published by
Excel Digital Press
P.O. Box 703978
Dallas, Texas 75370-3978
www.exceldigitalpress.com

ISBN 0-9749202-5-8

Cover Design and Diagrams by Kevin Hurley

Dedication

To my dad who faithfully guided me and taught me that there is no greater success than being true to biblical values and principles.

Contents

Acknowledgments vii

Foreword ix

Introduction x

Part One
The Keys to Excellence

1. Dad's Secret 6
2. Salient Elements (the Secret) of an Excellent Organization 14
3. A Few Definitions and Presuppositions 18

Part Two
The Beyond Babel Model

4. The Foundation: A Biblical Worldview 28
5. Equally Yoked Senior Leaders 54
6. Strategic Planning 86
7. Executional Excellence 110
8. Excellence Validated by the Customer: The Ultimate Test 138

Part Three
The Beyond Babel Model in Practice

9. Does the Beyond Babel Model Really Work? 154
10. Is the Beyond Babel Model
    Consistent with Empirical Research? 168
11. Why Are There So Few Excellent Organizations? 182
12. Can You Build an Excellent Organization? 192

In Summary 204

Appendices
I. Frequently Asked Questions (FAQs) 212
II. More Comparisons 214

About the Author 229
For Further Study 230

Acknowledgments

As with any author, there are many people who have helped to shape my life, and, therefore, this book. It is difficult to properly acknowledge all of them; however, I will make an attempt to express my deep appreciation to just a few of the vast number of people who have invested their time and ideas in me.

First and foremost is my wife, Carol. The faithful loving partner of my youth who is always there for me and never fails to speak truth to me. One of the greatest acts of love is speaking truth to another. She is indeed a loving, caring wife.

Next are my parents, William F. and Lorene E. Chester, who, like my wife, are always there for me. I so appreciate their love, support, and counsel. In particular, I want to thank my dad who mentored me in business and believed in me enough to give me an opportunity to be part of the family business. This experience was a vital component of my maturing process for which I will be forever grateful.

My wife's parents, Howard and Ann Prier, have been model in-laws. Like my own parents, they, too, have been very supportive through the years. I so appreciate the spiritual heritage they passed on to me, which provides an anchor to my soul.

There are numerous teachers who helped me to understand the Bible and appreciate it as the central source of authority in my life. The most important of these men was Dr. S. Lewis Johnson, a man who believed in me and invested much time teaching me theology. Shortly after Dr. Johnson's death in January of 2004, Dr. Bruce Waltke stated that Dr. Johnson was the best Bible expositor alive in the last half of the twentieth century. I concur and am honored to have been under his tutelage. In addition, I want to thank the many other Bible teachers who invested in me, men such as Bill McRae, Bob Deffinbaugh, Tony Emge, Ed Blum, and Dudley Hall. Each of these men was instrumental in helping me gain a deeper understanding of the treasures in the Bible.

During the past decade, the most significant man in my life has been Dennis Peacocke, a Christian philosopher similar to Francis Schaeffer. Dennis challenges me to go deeper and to think outside the box. It was his encouragement and teaching that stimulated much of the work that led to the message of this book.

During some of the most difficult times of my life, Dr. Jim Syvrud was a dear friend. He is one of the sweetest and most sensitive men that I have ever had the privilege of knowing. His loving support helped me and my family through very troubling times.

The people that helped to critique the manuscript of this book were marvelous. My lead editor, Janene MacIvor, was outstanding. Also, Dom Perrotta, Gary Cooper, Jim Hummel, Gene Painter, Josh Brannon, and Bob Deffinbaugh were invaluable resources to help me finalize the manuscript. To these and the many others who helped, thank you so much.

James Ryle, one of the most gifted communicators that I have ever known, suggested the title of the book. Thank you, James.

Finally, I would be remiss if I didn't acknowledge my professors in the physics department at the University of Texas, particularly Dr. Bengtson, Dr. Oakes, and Dr. Little, who taught me so much about the marvelous principles of the material universe. In some way, these principles correlate to the intangible universe. Exploring and understanding this correlation is a driving force in my life.

To all the above men and women who have helped me, believed in me, supported me, and stood with me, I say, ever so inadequately, *thank you*! I pray that this book will be a source of satisfaction and accomplishment for them, as they played a vital role in making the book a reality.

Most of all, I thank the Lord for orchestrating the circumstances of my life to enable me to write this book and to offer it as a sacrifice of praise to Him.

Gerald R. Chester, Ph.D.
November 2004

Foreword

Gerald Chester is a very serious Christian in serious pursuit of God's building patterns. Trained in the "hard science" of physics, he brings to the art of business management and organization an inquiring mind and a commitment to understand and quantify results. The book you are about to read reflects all these characteristics. Disciples are "disciplined learners" and Gerald is all of that.

It is sometimes difficult to assess privately, let alone publicly, as in this foreword, a friend's creative work. My association with Gerald, both privately and in our common work together, makes this task both easy and enjoyable. All students of the art of building a business God's way will find this book very, very helpful. However, beyond all that, and in some ways even more importantly, Gerald endeavors to live out the truths he gives with clarity and insight in this book. Therefore, this work has moral authority, the most important of all leadership characteristics. It authenticates his observations.

Out of this rigorous quest for excellence, Dr. Chester has given us all the benefit of his studied findings after many years of participating in business ventures and subsequent consulting with numerous companies. He is also a voracious reader of materials salient to his passion for businesspeople and organizations that reflect Christ and His Kingdom in life in general, and the marketplace in particular. Welcome to the benefits of his process. □Please read, enjoy, and practice!

Dennis Peacocke
November 2004

Introduction

The earliest group project recorded in the Bible is the attempt to build the Tower of Babel.[1] The sponsors of this project were unified in purpose to build a tower to the heavens. There was clear and common communication, a necessity for any major endeavor. They selected a level place that would support such a structure. To build a tall structure required that it be erected perpendicular to the ground. As the structure was built, deviations from perpendicular would be exaggerated, creating stability problems. To minimize deviations, the builders used brick instead of stone. Brick can be made uniform in size, whereas stone is naturally irregular. Initially the project enjoyed success; the project, however, was doomed to failure. The sponsors of the project had the wrong motive: they were seeking to exalt themselves, which is inconsistent with God's purposes.

There are many lessons to be learned from the Tower of Babel incident. The sponsors of the project adroitly used several key principles. They understood the critical nature of unified communications and a proper foundation. Also, they understood the importance of using the correct technology, bricks instead of stones. But they failed to understand the critical nature of motive. God is interested in man's heart.[2] The Bible states that God *"detests the proud of heart . . . they will not go unpunished."*[3] God's judgment at Babel was to disrupt the communication, which stopped the project.

It is my objective to go beyond Babel. This means that we must learn from the mistake at Babel. It is not enough to build great projects based on the unity of the sponsors, a solid foundation, and the best technology. We must also have the right motive rooted in humility and submission to the God of the Bible, the Creator of the universe. Humility means that we humans don't define reality but submit to God's definition of reality. In other words, we see reality through God's eyes or His worldview. This means that organizations need to seek God's perspective on what projects to build, when to build them, and how to build them. Discovering how to build God's way is a process of developing a philosophy of organizational behavior and practices, including principles and values, aligned with the revelation of God given in the Bible.

This book is about how organizations can enjoy success through alignment with God's perspective. The typical book on organizational behavior is either a report on the principles practiced by a highly regarded organization such as Neiman Marcus, a research project by someone like Jim Collins (*Good to Great*) or a philosophical discussion by a noted pundit such as Peter Drucker. The principles presented are discovered pragmatically. *Pragmatism* is a worldview that defines truth and reality based on what works. This is the worldview of most organizations. The fact that pragmatism is so ubiquitous is a testimony to the complexity of managing organizations. It is also an acknowledgment that there is no perceived definitive handbook on organizational behavior.

Beyond Babel offers a different worldview for assessing organizational behavior. In particular, it offers a model for organizational excellence based on a *biblical worldview*, which I call the Beyond Babel Model. For most people, the Bible, at best, provides personal ethical guidance. Some esteem it highly, but very few would consider using the Bible as an authoritative source of principles and practices to manage organizations. *Beyond Babel* assumes that the Creator of the universe provided the Bible to guide us in all areas of life,[4] including organizational principles and practices. In other words, my presupposition is that the God of the Bible created the universe, and that He also defined the rules for all the games of life—personal life, family life, church life, business life, and community life.

The immediate challenge in using the Bible as a handbook of organizational principles and practices is *dualism*. Dualism is the assumed bifurcation of spiritual and material reality. This book does not embrace dualism; rather it embraces the opposite, which is *integration*. Integration is a holistic approach to life based on the presupposition that the Bible is God's revelation to man and that the Bible speaks definitively and authoritatively to every jurisdiction, including business and government.

Hermeneutically, this book assumes that the Bible is to be interpreted grammatically and historically. *Grammatically* means that the various types of literature contained in the Bible are to be recognized and interpreted accordingly. *Historically* means that the Bible's historical setting is to be considered in its interpretation.

Every organization enjoys the opportunity to use the Bible, as illuminated by the Holy Spirit, as a source of principles and practices to govern its organizational behavior. To glean these principles and practices, it is understood that the Bible reveals the character and nature of God and how God builds. It is assumed that God's principles and practices for building provide us with a model for how He wants us to build. Therefore, when organizations align with God by embracing His principles and practices, the result is outstanding organizational performance.

Pragmatic experience can lead to alignment with the Bible. For example, many organizations practice the Golden Rule[5] not because it is biblical, but because it works. For most organizations, alignment with God's principles occurs because the organizations pragmatically discover that God's principles work even though the organizations may not realize the origin of the principles. It would be even better if organizations practiced the Golden Rule because it was biblical, not simply because the principle works.

Since alignment with God is the predicate for enduring organizational success, it follows that an organization's success is proportional to its alignment with God's principles.

This book presents the Beyond Babel Model of organizational excellence, which is rooted in the Bible. In my work with organizations, I seek those that desire to engage in this approach to organizational management. Some organizations merely give lip service to employing biblical principles. Others try to practice it, but lack biblical knowledge and understanding. And still others have achieved superior results by embracing biblical principles. I find great joy in working with organizations that eagerly embrace and practice biblical principles. It is a delight to see these organizations move "Beyond Babel." What a joy it would be if this became an ubiquitous reality.

Notes

1. Genesis 11:1–9.
2. Proverbs 17:3.
3. Proverbs 16:5.
4. 2 Peter 1:3.
5. Matthew 7:12.

Beyond Babel Model

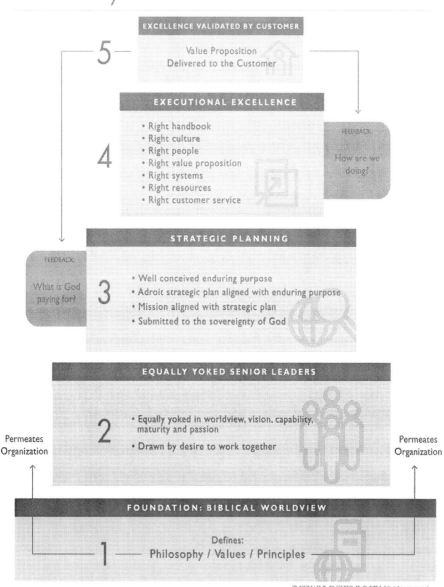

5 — EXCELLENCE VALIDATED BY CUSTOMER

Value Proposition
Delivered to the Customer

4 EXECUTIONAL EXCELLENCE

- Right handbook
- Right culture
- Right people
- Right value proposition
- Right systems
- Right resources
- Right customer service

FEEDBACK:

How are we doing?

3 STRATEGIC PLANNING

- Well conceived enduring purpose
- Adroit strategic plan aligned with enduring purpose
- Mission aligned with strategic plan
- Submitted to the sovereignty of God

FEEDBACK:

What is God paying for?

2 EQUALLY YOKED SENIOR LEADERS

- Equally yoked in worldview, vision, capability, maturity and passion
- Drawn by desire to work together

Permeates Organization

Permeates Organization

1 FOUNDATION: BIBLICAL WORLDVIEW

Defines:
Philosophy / Values / Principles

PART ONE

The Keys
to Excellence

Do you see a man skilled in his work?
He will serve before kings;
he will not serve before obscure men.

Virtually every organization that I have served as a consultant expresses the desire to build an excellent organization. Despite this expressed desire, I find very few organizations that enjoy the distinction of being truly great. We humans seem to be long on words but short on actions.

So what are the keys to building a truly great organization? The starting point is great people. After all, organizations are nothing more than two or more people who have joined together to accomplish a mission.

But how does one find great people? Great people are those who have wrestled with and adroitly answered one of the most vexing questions of life: Why am I here? To answer this question with a depth of insight, one must deal with the issue of being a created individual and submitting to the purposes of the Creator. The impact of this statement is enormous and exceeds the scope of this book. Nevertheless, a fundamental assumption of this book is that great organizations are built by people who understand the reason for their being.

Given this presupposition, we can now embark on discovering the keys to excellence. People who are walking in their individual destinies build truly great world-class organizations and, either wittingly or unwittingly, discover and practice the keys to excellence. This book purports to articulate these keys. When these keys are practiced, the result is world-class organizations delivering world-class products, widely recognized and valued. These organizations will be very skilled and will stand before kings.

Notes

Epigraph: Proverbs 22:29

Beyond Babel Model

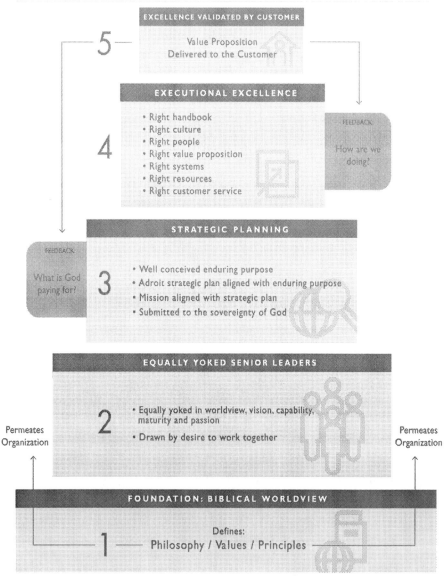

EXCELLENCE VALIDATED BY CUSTOMER

5 — Value Proposition
Delivered to the Customer

EXECUTIONAL EXCELLENCE

4
- Right handbook
- Right culture
- Right people
- Right value proposition
- Right systems
- Right resources
- Right customer service

FEEDBACK:

How are we doing?

STRATEGIC PLANNING

FEEDBACK:

What is God paying for?

3
- Well conceived enduring purpose
- Adroit strategic plan aligned with enduring purpose
- Mission aligned with strategic plan
- Submitted to the sovereignty of God

EQUALLY YOKED SENIOR LEADERS

2
- Equally yoked in worldview, vision, capability, maturity and passion
- Drawn by desire to work together

Permeates
Organization

Permeates
Organization

FOUNDATION: BIBLICAL WORLDVIEW

1 — Defines:
Philosophy / Values / Principles

Dad's Secret

Driving my father home from the restaurant where we celebrated his eightieth birthday over lunch, I was inspired to tell him that I knew his secret. I could tell that he was somewhat puzzled by my comment, so I decided to give him a hint: "Dad, do you remember the story that you told me about having to lay off some workers during the early days of your business?" He still didn't remember, so I went on to tell him what he had told me some years before.

In 1949, he and a partner started United Plumbing Company in Dallas, Texas. Times were difficult for young companies then. The two partners worked hard and enjoyed moderate success. They were not, however, flush with cash. At one point business slowed and they were forced to lay off some of their laborers. In those days, United Plumbing was installing residential plumbing and used laborers to dig ditches, since affordable ditching machines did not exist. Manual labor was the technology of the day. These laborers were unskilled, but they took pride in digging ditches. As a very young boy, I remember seeing some of these ditches and being amazed at how neatly the ditches were dug; even the sides were straight. Though digging ditches was considered a lowly job, Dad respected these men for their pride of workmanship, dedication, and work ethic.

The day came when the layoff was to take place. Dad's partner's approach was to simply call the men in and tell them that they were no longer needed. The directness of his partner's approach was too impersonal for Dad. He insisted on talking to each man individually and expressing his heartfelt appreciation and his deep regret that the layoff was neccessary. From this and other experiences, Dad and his partner realized that they could not continue in business together. Soon thereafter, Dad bought his partner out of the business.

After reminding Dad of this story, I again said to him, "I know your secret." I told him the secret was simply a philosophy and value system that put others first. He had practiced it with great skill and built a wonderful company. I told him that I had been studying organizations as a consultant for a long time. (My experience includes a stint running Dad's business plus working with more than seventy different organizations as a consultant, and reading numerous books and articles on companies widely regarded as excellent organizations.) I told Dad that my experience had proved the value of his "secret" again and again.

> **I TOLD HIM THE SECRET WAS SIMPLY A PHILOSOPHY AND VALUE SYSTEM THAT PUT OTHERS FIRST.**

Dad launched into a monologue articulating the principles and values that he practiced throughout the years. First his humility came forth, as he prefaced his comments with the qualifier that he had made many mistakes. Then he went on to articulate how important it is to treat people right, to build an excellent reputation, to do outstanding work, and to not focus on money—as money will take care of itself. He went on to reminisce about how hard it was to come from nothing to build a business. There were many days when the trials and tribulations of the business were overwhelming. The heartache and headaches were difficult; nevertheless, he stayed the course and finished the race.

Dad was born in Coppell, Texas, on December 27, 1922, to a sharecropper named Lewis P. Chester and his wife, Bessie. In those days, Coppell was a small farming community. The farmers primarily raised cotton. Dad remembers picking cotton as a young boy and times when he went to bed hungry and had no shoes. During the summer, he would move his bed outside seeking relief from the heat buildup in the house. As soon as he could, he went to work. As a teenager, he went to school by day, worked in the afternoons and evenings, and studied when he could. He worked at gas stations and industrial plants doing hard manual labor. After Pearl Harbor, he joined the navy to serve his country and learned pipe fitting, which he thoroughly enjoyed. After the war, he sought to build on his interest in piping and learned the plumbing trade. In 1949, he and his partner started their plumbing contracting business.

After Dad bought out his partner, his company struggled for several years. Dad worked hard to get business and to build a great reputation. There was much sacrifice before the business thrived. Soon his brothers and brothers-in-law were working for his company. Through the years, nephews and one of his sons (that would be me) would work for his company. The company became a vehicle of great blessings for the family.

Dad possessed a strong work ethic and a keen sense of responsibility. In his worldview, a man should provide for his family. He did this with great skill and integrity. As with all of us, his worldview defined his value system. A conservative, traditional biblical worldview was the norm in this country in the 1920s and '30s. America honored the God of Christianity at home and at work. People embraced honesty, hard work, integrity, faithfulness, fidelity, kindness, generosity, and so forth. Your word was your bond. Divorce was uncommon because marriage was viewed as a lifelong commitment. Premarital sex was taboo, and pregnancies out of wedlock were rare.

During the decade of the '30s, the most formative years of Dad's early life, economic depression gripped the country. This experience taught him the value of work and being a good steward of what he earned. Throughout the depression, many men traveled the country looking for work. As these men came through towns like Coppell, the local families would frequently provide them hospitality—teaching Dad to be kind and generous to others in need. His family was large: there were five sisters and three brothers, including Dad. He learned to respect others and be part of a team. My grandfather's work consisted of low-paying jobs; the family had very little in the way of worldly possessions, but it was a happy family and Dad learned to be content with little. I am sure that he already had respect for authority, but his experience in the navy in World War II surely reinforced this value.

By the time he started his business in 1949, Dad's value system was deeply rooted. He could not separate himself from his values; they were at the core of his being and guided every decision he made. Some of his values were and still are a strong work ethic, a high regard for all people, a strong commitment to excellence, adroit stewardship of all resources, and a high level of integrity. Dad has never been able to relate to situational ethics, which is rooted in a presupposition that there are no absolute values. He knows that God defines values and that we will all give an account for what we do in this life. Dad would not lie or steal or cheat anyone. Such conduct was anathema to him. He was so strong in his core values that a handshake with him was all that was needed. Legal documents were superfluous, as he consistently exceeded both the letter and spirit of his agreements.

DAD HAS NEVER BEEN ABLE TO RELATE TO SITUATIONAL ETHICS, WHICH IS ROOTED IN A PRESUPPOSITION THAT THERE ARE NO ABSOLUTE VALUES.

Not surprisingly, Dad built an outstanding reputation in the construction industry in Dallas. Through the years, he developed strong loyal business relationships. Customers knew they would get excellent work at a fair price. They knew that if Dad gave them a time commitment, it would be honored or he would call before the deadline to explain. And when he couldn't, he would go the extra mile to make it right with the customer. Vendors knew that they would be paid properly and promptly. They would not be abused or lied to. Workers knew that they would be treated well. Fair wages, good working conditions, proper tools and equipment, and competent management were always the hallmark of the organization. On more than one occasion, I remember Dad helping workers who got into legal, financial, or family trouble. It didn't matter what the problem was; Dad always took care of his workers.

Dad's company was run conservatively and was consistently profitable. Resources were managed with skill. Anything that could be recycled was. Materials were bought in large quantities to get the best price available. The warehouse was always neat and organized, so that warehouse damage was minimal and shortages of stock items were rare. When Dad needed to buy capital assets, such as trucks and expensive equipment, he saved the money. Seldom did he go into debt, as he disdained it. Once his business was established, he always had reserves to weather economic storms.

Once the foundation of the company was solid, Dad strategically positioned the company to move into commercial and industrial plumbing work. As that prospered, he also moved into air conditioning and sheet metal work. All of this growth was carefully and conservatively managed so that the company was never seriously at risk as the business expanded. Dad followed the principles of building on a solid foundation and doing it little by little.

Doesn't this sound like an excellent organization? Customers and vendors wanted to do business with Dad. Workers loved Dad and were loyal to him. Within twenty years of being in business, the company was known as one of the best plumbing and air-conditioning contractors in the Dallas–Fort Worth Metroplex. And it was all because of Dad's unwavering commitment to, and practice of, biblical values. This is how one builds an excellent organization.

Researchers Discover That Dad Was Right

Business researchers are discovering that the values-centered principles that enabled Dad to build an excellent organization are universal principles. Leonard Berry is the author of *Discovering the Soul of Service*.[1] In this book, Berry studied fourteen companies in a variety of industries—public and private, large and small. All of these companies are well known for delivering excellent products and services. Berry wanted to discover the common ingredients. What is it that makes an organization truly excellent? He discovered eight common traits, but more important, he discovered the secret. The secret is what he calls humane values.[2] He cites seven core values[3]— excellence, joy, innovation, respect, teamwork, social profit, and integrity. I did not find in Berry's book any discussion about where these values come from; he was very clear, however, that great organizations are built on great values.

So where do great values come from? Great values are defined by a biblical worldview. A biblical worldview is a perspective on life that is rooted in the teachings of the Bible. The seven core values cited by Berry are all rooted in the Bible. The Bible exhorts us to work as if the Lord were our boss, which implies that we need to work with excellence.[4] Joy is a characteristic of one who is filled with the Holy Spirit.[5] Innovation is about not resting on one's laurels, but rather always seeking to improve.[6] Respect is regarding and treating others as valuable. Every human being is valuable because we are all created in the image of God.[7] Teamwork is the natural by-product of realizing that we are gifted in different ways and that any successful organization requires a variety of gifts working together to achieve its mission.[8] Social profit is the fruit of looking beyond an organization's self-interest to the good of the whole.[9] Finally, integrity means that one walks the talk.[10]

BIBLICAL PRINCIPLES UNDERLIE ORGANIZATIONAL EXCELLENCE.

Berry is not alone in discovering that biblical principles underlie organizational excellence; however, he does not note a source for these principles. Noted business pundits, such as Peter Drucker, Jim Collins, and Tom Peters, extol principles that facilitate excellent, enduring organizations. All of the efficacious principles that facilitate organizational excellence can be found in the Bible—the "owner's manual" for every organization. This should not be surprising.

IF GOD CREATED THE UNIVERSE, IT IS ONLY LOGICAL THAT HE WOULD DEFINE THE WAY THAT THE UNIVERSE SHOULD RUN, INCLUDING BUSINESS.

If God created the universe, it is only logical that He would define the way that the universe should run, including business. Therefore, honest objective business research should discover principles that are in harmony with the Bible— and many times clearly expressed in the Bible. The Bible is an exciting resource for discovering how to build enduring excellent organizations.

Notes

1. Leonard L. Berry, *Discovering the Soul of Service* (NY: The Free Press, 1999).

2. Ibid., 17.

3. Ibid., 23.

4. Colossians 3:23.

5. Galatians 5:22.

6. Philippians 3:13.

7. Genesis 1:26.

8. 1 Corinthians 12.

9. Philippians 2:4.

10. James 2:26.

Beyond Babel Model

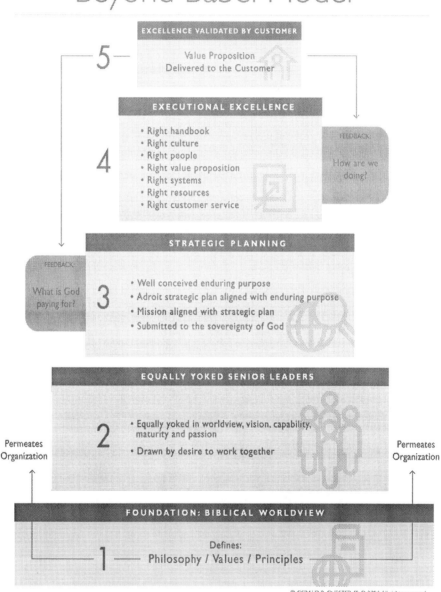

EXCELLENCE VALIDATED BY CUSTOMER

5 — Value Proposition
Delivered to the Customer

EXECUTIONAL EXCELLENCE

4
- Right handbook
- Right culture
- Right people
- Right value proposition
- Right systems
- Right resources
- Right customer service

FEEDBACK

How are we doing?

STRATEGIC PLANNING

FEEDBACK

What is God paying for?

3
- Well conceived enduring purpose
- Adroit strategic plan aligned with enduring purpose
- Mission aligned with strategic plan
- Submitted to the sovereignty of God

EQUALLY YOKED SENIOR LEADERS

2
- Equally yoked in worldview, vision, capability, maturity and passion
- Drawn by desire to work together

Permeates
Organization

Permeates
Organization

FOUNDATION: BIBLICAL WORLDVIEW

1 — Defines:
Philosophy / Values / Principles

Salient Elements (the Secret) of an Excellent Organization

One of the unspoken assumptions about business is that it operates by its own set of rules. What are these rules? Where did they come from? How does one discover them? The answer for many people to the "what" and "how" questions is: whatever pragmatically works. The answer to the "where" question is not relevant. People bifurcate business from the rest of life as if it does not relate to anything else. A business, however, is simply an organization. And as in any organization there must be rules and processes to facilitate and enable the business to achieve excellence.

> **PEOPLE BIFURCATE BUSINESS FROM THE REST OF LIFE AS IF IT DOES NOT RELATE TO ANYTHING ELSE.**

If one believes that the Bible is the inspired word of God, and therefore God's revelation to man about His creation, it follows that the principles that make organizations great should be God's principles. In other words, if God created the game of life, He also created the rules of the game.

Based on this presupposition, it follows that the Bible should provide guidance to organizations regarding how to—among other things—treat people, solve problems, serve others, divide labor, build leaders, develop relationships, manage resources, attain a good reputation, define success, view money, utilize technology, select investments, articulate mission statements, develop strategic plans, keep score, finance projects, define organizational cultures, face truth, execute with excellence, and validate reality. The Bible should also provide the value system by which the organization functions. If we indeed accept the proposition that the Bible is God's revelation to His material creation, there should be no aspect of business for which the Bible does not provide guidance.

To properly utilize the Bible, it is important to understand the nature of the Bible. The Bible is not a systematic theology or a textbook. It is a compilation of books written under the inspiration of the Holy Spirit[1] by various people, compiled during the course of history, and historically recognized by godly church leaders as revelation from God. The Bible, also called "special revelation" by theologians, contains revelation as to the nature and purpose of God. The physical universe is known as "general revelation." Man's responsibility is to subdue the earth (or physical universe),[2] which means to study, understand, and master general revelation from the perspective of a biblical worldview. Therefore, all literature written by man should contribute to the knowledge base of man in our collective quest to obey God's command to subdue the universe.

An excellent organization is one that looks

> IF WE INDEED ACCEPT THE PROPOSITION THAT THE BIBLE IS GOD'S REVELATION TO HIS MATERIAL CREATION, THERE SHOULD BE NO ASPECT OF BUSINESS FOR WHICH THE BIBLE DOES NOT PROVIDE GUIDANCE.

> AN EXCELLENT ORGANIZATION IS ONE THAT LOOKS TO THE BIBLE TO PROVIDE THE PHILOSOPHY, PRINCIPLES, AND VALUES NEEDED TO OPERATE IN ALIGNMENT WITH GOD'S PERSPECTIVE.

to the Bible to provide the philosophy, principles, and values needed to operate in alignment with God's perspective. If God blesses philosophical and practical alignment with Himself, an organization that adopts and practices the values and operating principles found in the Bible should maximize its opportunity to enjoy enduring success. The validation of an organization's alignment with God is found by inspecting the organization's fruit. If the organization produces superior products and services, as measured by its customers, this suggests that the organization must be aligned, to some degree, with a biblical worldview. The Bible teaches that a tree is recognized by its fruit.[3] The fruit of excellent products and services surely reveals that there is an excellent organization producing such fruit.

Tying organizational success to alignment with biblical principles begs the question: What about sweat shops and other organizations that abuse people and/or break the law? Such organizations may enjoy some short-term financial success; long term, however, such business practices out of sync with the Bible will not endure. The Bible states:

...a sinner's wealth is stored up for the righteous.[4]

The Key Elements of the Beyond Babel Model

Based on the assumption that the Bible is the handbook for organizational behavior, just as it is for personal behavior, I propose that organizational excellence is built on the following five key elements:

1. Biblical worldview
2. Equally yoked senior leaders
3. Strategic planning
4. Executional excellence
5. Customer validation

It is my assertion that the Beyond Babel Model of excellence will lead any organization or individual to world-class performance.

Notes

1. 2 Timothy 3:16.   3. Matthew 12:33.

2. Genesis 1:26–28.   4. Proverbs 13:22.

Beyond Babel Model

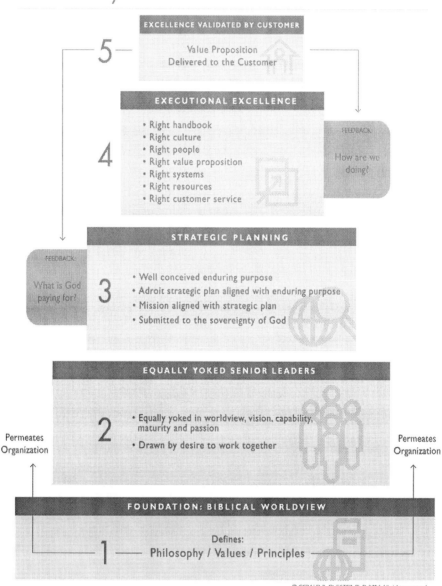

EXCELLENCE VALIDATED BY CUSTOMER

5

Value Proposition
Delivered to the Customer

EXECUTIONAL EXCELLENCE

4

- Right handbook
- Right culture
- Right people
- Right value proposition
- Right systems
- Right resources
- Right customer service

FEEDBACK
How are we doing?

STRATEGIC PLANNING

FEEDBACK
What is God paying for?

3

- Well conceived enduring purpose
- Adroit strategic plan aligned with enduring purpose
- Mission aligned with strategic plan
- Submitted to the sovereignty of God

EQUALLY YOKED SENIOR LEADERS

2

- Equally yoked in worldview, vision, capability, maturity and passion
- Drawn by desire to work together

Permeates Organization

Permeates Organization

FOUNDATION: BIBLICAL WORLDVIEW

1

Defines:
Philosophy / Values / Principles

A Few Definitions and Presuppositions

Before beginning the discussion of the Beyond Babel Model, I want to define some key terms and articulate my most significant presuppositions.

Definition and Purpose of an Organization

David Packard asserted that an organization is simply a group of people that exists to "accomplish something collectively that they could not accomplish separately."[1] As good as this definition may be, it is, nonetheless, incomplete. Organizations may also exist to accelerate the accomplishment of tasks. For example, I may be able to build a house, but it can be built much faster if I have help, and if time is money, it can be built cheaper as well.

Organizations may also exist to facilitate quality. For example, one way that quality is achieved is through repetition. If I build a house by myself, I have to do the work of all the trades. However, if someone performs the same trade every day, it's unlikely that I could perform any given trade as well as the person who specializes in that trade. Hence, organizations facilitate the quality achieved through division of labor. I would therefore assert that an organization is a group of people that exists to execute a mission better, faster, and cheaper than could be done by an individual.

Biblically, an organization is a vehicle for stewardship. God owns the earth[2] and has charged man with the responsibility for ruling (or stewarding)[3] the earth. Therefore, it is wisdom on the part of man to form organizations to efficiently execute this stewardship.

Definition of Success

Success is defined as alignment with God's purposes; that is, God desires that we humans, His created beings, submit to His rulership in our lives. The ultimate example of this is Jesus and His death on the cross. As bad as it was, that event is the most significant event in human history. Its significance is found in what God was doing through it, mainly redeeming man from sin.[4] Many times alignment with God's purposes does not include a large financial blessing. Consider,

> **AN ORGANIZATION IS A GROUP OF PEOPLE THAT EXISTS TO EXECUTE A MISSION BETTER, FASTER, AND CHEAPER THAN COULD BE DONE BY AN INDIVIDUAL.**

for example, Jesus, who at least partially, lived off charity,[5] which indicates that He was not wealthy financially. On the other hand, the Bible records that at times divine favor was displayed by financial favor, such as with David.[6] Therefore, contrary to the belief of many, financial growth is one indicator of divine favor but not the only indicator. The indicator of success, from God's perspective, is alignment with God's purposes. Because God's purposes will prevail, only those organizations and projects aligned with Him will last.

> **THE INDICATOR OF SUCCESS, FROM GOD'S PERSPECTIVE, IS ALIGNMENT WITH GOD'S PURPOSES.**

Corollaries to success are terms such as *enduring* and *world-class*. *Enduring* refers to something that lasts for long periods of time because God blesses the project and/or organization. *World-class* implies work that is excellent or of the highest quality, which implies that there is nothing better.

Definition of Philosophy, Values, and Principles

Throughout the book you will find references to "philosophy, values, and principles." *Philosophy* refers to wisdom and is an expression of the worldview of a person or organization.

Values are the ethical qualities that a person or organization embraces, such as truth, integrity, humility, excellence, and love. Values are a by-product of worldview. For example, if one's worldview (or philosophy) is rooted in the assumption that the Bible is God's revelation to man, one would then search the Bible to find biblical values. Such a search would surely reveal that the highest biblical value is love;[7] hence, one seeking to be true to one's philosophy would embrace love as the highest value.

Principles are the operating practices that practically express the philosophy and values of a person or organization. For example, if one embraces love as a value, a wonderful principle that embodies and expresses love is the Golden Rule (do to others as you would have them do to you).[8]

Presuppositions

The starting point for developing any worldview or philosophy is always a person's *presuppositions*. Everyone has presuppositions, assumptions, or beliefs that by definition cannot be proved, which means that everyone is a person of faith. These presuppositions are the starting point for developing a comprehensive, integrated view of reality. Some of my presuppositions are as follows:

EVERYONE IS A PERSON OF FAITH.

- Reality exists and is knowable;

- God exists, is knowable, and chooses to reveal Himself to mankind in creation (general revelation) and the Bible (special revelation);

- The Bible is to be interpreted grammatically and historically in accordance to the various types of literature found therein;

- Man exists and has senses that provide accurate data about reality (the Bible and creation);

- God created the laws of reasoning, knowledge, and logic— specifically, the laws of noncontradiction and reproducibility; and

- Man's mind can process the data from the Bible and creation to comprehend knowledge about God.

Given this set of assumptions, one can study the Bible to develop a holistic view of reality. Data empirically gleaned from general revelation (the physical universe) is interpreted so as to be consistent with the Bible. Specifically, one can develop a best-practices model of organizational excellence based on biblical principles by pragmatically studying excellent organizations.

To validate this perspective, one can pose a test. If the God of the Bible created the universe, then it follows that He created all the principles by which the universe operates. It logically follows that for created beings to thrive in God's creation, they must conform to God's principles. Therefore, researchers who empirically study organizational performance to determine the best practices that lead to world-class performance should find that the principles that facilitate organizational excellence are consistent with the Bible. My thesis is, that is the case.

With these definitions and presuppositions in mind, let us launch into the Beyond Babel Model.

Notes

1. J. Collins and J. Porras, *Built to Last* (NY: HarperBusiness, 1997), 58.

2. Psalms 24:1.

3. Genesis 1:26–28.

4. 1 Corinthians 15:3.

5. Luke 8:1–3.

6. 1 Chronicles 29:28.

7. Matthew 22:36-40.

8. Matthew 7:12.

Beyond Babel Model

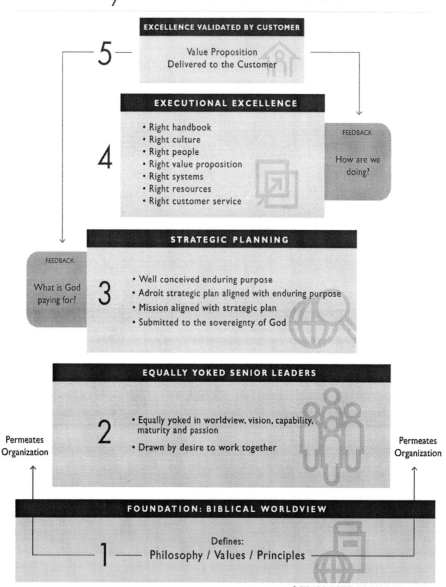

EXCELLENCE VALIDATED BY CUSTOMER

— 5 —

Value Proposition
Delivered to the Customer

EXECUTIONAL EXCELLENCE

4

- Right handbook
- Right culture
- Right people
- Right value proposition
- Right systems
- Right resources
- Right customer service

FEEDBACK:

How are we doing?

STRATEGIC PLANNING

FEEDBACK:

What is God paying for?

3

- Well conceived enduring purpose
- Adroit strategic plan aligned with enduring purpose
- Mission aligned with strategic plan
- Submitted to the sovereignty of God

EQUALLY YOKED SENIOR LEADERS

2

- Equally yoked in worldview, vision, capability, maturity and passion
- Drawn by desire to work together

Permeates Organization

Permeates Organization

FOUNDATION: BIBLICAL WORLDVIEW

1

Defines:
Philosophy / Values / Principles

PART TWO

The Beyond Babel Model

Whatever you do, do it all for the glory of God.

The Beyond Babel Model is about bringing glory to God in the way that organizations operate. In the story of the Tower of Babel in Genesis 11, the project sponsors were skilled in planning and executing the project. The starting point was unity of purpose: self-glorification. They were adroit planners. An appropriate location was found: a flat plain that would provide a stable foundation on which they could build. They used the most current and appropriate technology: regularly shaped bricks instead of irregularly shaped stones. Communication was clear: they worked as one people, which meant that personal agendas were subordinated to the purpose of the whole.

A KEY LESSON OF THE TOWER OF BABEL IS THAT SELF-GLORIFICATION AND GLORIFYING GOD ARE MUTUALLY EXCLUSIVE.

Other than the illicit purpose of self-glorification, all of the operating practices were commendable: thoughtful planning, an appropriate location and technology, clear communications, and unity. But the illicit purpose was their Achilles heel. Over the long term, God does not bless organizations that embrace illicit purposes. He requires us to glorify Him. We glorify Him by obeying Him. Such actions by us are the predicate for long-term blessing and success. As previously defined, success is obedience to Him. As we obey God, we glorify God.

A key lesson of the Tower of Babel is that self-glorification and glorifying God are mutually exclusive. One can do one or the other but not both simultaneously. Seeking self-glorification is idolatry, which violates the Ten Commandments.[1] Therefore, to go beyond Babel means that one builds organizations seeking to glorify God, and God alone, which means that one looks to God to define the philosophy, values, and principles required to build organizations.

The Beyond Babel Model is intended to challenge you to glorify God by building organizations that reflect His philosophy, values, and principles.

Notes

Epigraph: 1 Corinthians 10:31.

1. Exodus 20.

Beyond Babel Model

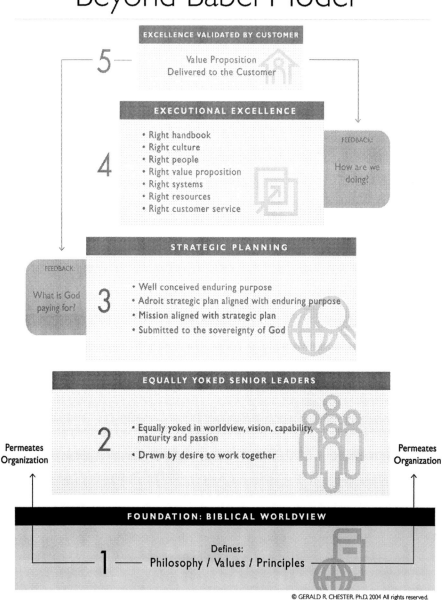

EXCELLENCE VALIDATED BY CUSTOMER

5 — Value Proposition
Delivered to the Customer

EXECUTIONAL EXCELLENCE

4
* Right handbook
* Right culture
* Right people
* Right value proposition
* Right systems
* Right resources
* Right customer service

FEEDBACK:
How are we
doing?

STRATEGIC PLANNING

FEEDBACK:
What is God
paying for?

3
* Well conceived enduring purpose
* Adroit strategic plan aligned with enduring purpose
* Mission aligned with strategic plan
* Submitted to the sovereignty of God

EQUALLY YOKED SENIOR LEADERS

2
* Equally yoked in worldview, vision, capability, maturity and passion
* Drawn by desire to work together

Permeates
Organization

Permeates
Organization

FOUNDATION: BIBLICAL WORLDVIEW

1 — Defines:
Philosophy / Values / Principles

The Foundation:
A Biblical Worldview

How Does *Worldview* Apply to Individuals and Organizations?

An Individual's Worldview

What does every human being have and use every day, but seldom talks about? The answer is a worldview. A worldview is a perspective of reality. It is a set of glasses through which each person interprets the events of life. Each of us has a set of presuppositions that form the foundation of our worldview. Presuppositions are beliefs that we accept to be true, and are not subject to empirical proof. For example, whether or not one believes that God exists is a presupposition. No one can prove the existence of God, nor can anyone prove that God does not exist. Each person, either wittingly or unwittingly, embraces a presupposition about the existence of God.

Once a presupposition is accepted, a person then interprets his or her perception of reality based on that presupposition. For example, how does one explain the origin of the universe? If one has an atheistic presupposition, then one looks for an explanation that does not include a creator. One of the reasons why evolution is so popular is that it provides such an explanation. On the other hand, if one has a theistic presupposition, then one explains the origin of the universe as the production of an intelligent creator.

A corollary to the discussion about creation is the issue of right and wrong. If one holds an atheistic presupposition, there is no standard of right and wrong. However, a theist views right and wrong as defined by the Creator. For example, consider the following quote:[1]

INSTINCT
What your heart thinks is great, is great.
The soul's emphasis is always right.
—Ralph Waldo Emerson

To say that the soul of any human is always right implies that there is such a reality as "right." A logically consistent atheistic humanist would contend that right only exists relative to each human; hence, there is no concept of absolutes that govern all men. A theistic, biblical perspective would qualify the meaning of "right" relative to God's definition, giving consideration to the reality of depravity as taught in the Bible.[2] Thus, a person can interpret Emerson's statement in different ways depending on his worldview.

> A WORLDVIEW IS A PERSPECTIVE OF REALITY. IT IS A SET OF GLASSES THROUGH WHICH EACH PERSON INTERPRETS THE EVENTS OF LIFE.

We humans habitually make statements in our daily lives that reflect our worldviews. At work, when we are frustrated with a problem and don't know what to do, we might say "whatever works," reflecting a pragmatic approach to problem solving. Where did this come from? It comes from our worldview. For those with a pragmatic worldview, the concept "whatever works" presumes the existence of both an end and a means to the end. Although one may have a vision of the end, the means must be discovered heuristically (by trial and error). Such a worldview reflects an ignorant or agnostic perspective about the nature of reality and how to solve the problem. In the context of a biblical worldview, however, pragmatism is an acknowledgement of man's limitations and God's incomprehensibility. The solution to the problem is to discover God's end and His means to achieving that end. Hence, the simple statement "whatever works" can be interpreted in different ways.

An Organization's Worldview

Just as each individual has a worldview, so also does each organization. The worldview of an organization defines truth and reality for the organization, since truth and reality emanate from the philosophy, values, and principles that the organization embraces.

A common by-product of the philosophy, values, and principles of an organization is the "corporate culture." Consider, for example, Wal-Mart—the retailing behemoth built by Sam Walton that started with a single store. The company is well known for its culture, which is the product of the philosophy, values, and principles of its founder. A key component of the philosophy of Wal-Mart is customer service.[3] To provide excellent customer service, the company embraces the value of people which is expressed in referring to workers as associates. And to train managers in the Wal-Mart culture, the company has Walton Institute. Sam Walton understood that his company's success was dependent on its ability to embrace and execute his philosophy, principles, and values.

> **JUST AS EACH INDIVIDUAL HAS A WORLDVIEW, SO ALSO DOES EACH ORGANIZATION.**

The culture of each organization is shaped by its worldview, which is defined by its senior leaders. How the organization treats its customers, workers, vendors, and so forth, is defined by its worldview. How the organization defines success is shaped by its worldview. This reality is easily seen in organizations. For example, it is common to hear comments about organizational behavior such as "that's the way we do it here." This statement simply reflects the culture of the organization, which is a direct reflection of the organization's worldview.

Every organization has a corporate culture—an accepted way of doing things. When I was at Texas Instruments (TI), every presentation was made with overhead slides. (I am sure they now use PowerPoint.) By adopting this practice, TI demonstrated that it valued visual communications. The Container Store puts the employee first and customers second under the belief that blessed workers will pass on the blessing to the customers. This emphasis leads to a positive culture. It is common to hear someone say "the TI way" or "the Container Store way," referring to the cultural practices of an organization.

Everyone within a given organization is expected to conform to the cultural norms of that organization. Where do these practices come from? Cultural norms come from the organization's worldview. At some point in the life of every organization, someone with influence shaped the worldview that is commonly embraced. Milton Hershey shaped the worldview of Hershey Chocolate, which values quality products and helping orphans. Clark Williams shaped the worldview of CenturyTel, which is so employee sensitive that it is highly unusual for an employee to lose his or her job. This is the CenturyTel way. IBM's culture embraces the importance of a person's career path to the point that no one is hired for a permanent position unless a career path can be mapped out in advance. If a position cannot be tied to an employee's career path, the position is filled by a contractor. This is the IBM way.

CONFLICT WITHIN AN ORGANIZATION OCCURS WHEN THE WORLDVIEW OF THE ORGANIZATION IS AT ODDS WITH THE WORLDVIEW OF AN INDIVIDUAL OR GROUP OF INDIVIDUALS.

Values consistent with a worldview must be internalized. It is very difficult to externally impose a worldview. Regardless of what people profess with their lips, in the end the reality of their worldview will manifest itself. Southwest Airlines understands this as well as anyone. They are nearly fanatical about protecting their corporate culture. Their mantra is "hire for attitude, train for skills."[4] By this they mean that attitudes that are rooted in worldview are not easily changed, but people can learn the skills needed for most jobs. A critical ingredient to Southwest's success is a harmonious workforce with common attitudes and perspectives.

Conflict within an organization occurs when the worldview of the organization is at odds with the worldview of an individual or group of individuals. Consider the following example:

> More than 3,000 law students in India protested official policies against cheating. They were upset at a policy that bans copying on exams, according to Australia's Courier-Mail newspaper. Things got violent after police were called to help confiscate all their cheat sheets. Some students blocked a highway and started burning tires. They claim copying answers is a tradition that authorities must respect. "We found almost all students carrying books and photo-copied notes hidden on their body," education official Radhanath Mishra told the paper. "We asked them to hand over all the illegally smuggled study materials. But they did not listen to us."[5]

While this may seem like an extreme case, it illustrates the fact that differences in values, and therefore worldview, lead to conflict. Conflict drains the energy and resources from organizations, which leads to inefficient production. Inefficient production does not lead to excellent organizations.

Researchers who seek to understand organizational excellence articulate the reality that a strong unchanging value system is at the core of organizational excellence. For example, note the comment: "The only truly reliable source of stability is a strong inner core and the willingness to change and adapt everything except that core."[6] Leonard Berry wrote, "Humane organizational values sustain human excellence."[7]

WHAT THESE RESEARCHERS ARE DISCOVERING IS THAT A STRONG MORAL UNCHANGEABLE WORLDVIEW PROVIDES THE FOUNDATION FOR ORGANIZATIONAL SUCCESS.

What these researchers are discovering is that a strong moral unchangeable worldview provides the foundation for organizational success. Note this comment by one researcher: "Leaders die, products become obsolete, markets change, new technologies emerge, management fads come and go, but core ideology [worldview] in a great company [or organization] endures as a source of guidance and inspiration."[8]

Worldview Options

Though the researchers are unified in the message that an unchanging or absolute value system is the foundation for sustained organizational excellence and success, they do not attempt to identify the origin of these values. One gets the impression that many researchers don't know where their values come from and are not interested in discerning the source. It is as if magically we are to know these values. Or perhaps they posit that these values are an integral part of each human being and are therefore intuitive. Regardless, I am not aware of a serious attempt by business researchers to understand the source of the value system that an organization must practice to achieve excellence. So where do these values come from? There are really only two options—inside of man or outside of man.

Internal Sources

The best illustration of a worldview that derives its values from sources inside of man is the humanist worldview. Humanists contend that man is the measure of all things.[9] Therefore, there are no principles or values that apply to every human being—no absolutes. Each person determines his or her own values and worldview.

This position seems inconsistent with the real world in which businesses must operate. Note the worldview reflected by the company American Standard as stated on its Web site: "American Standard Companies recently launched a new Code of Conduct and Ethics that sets high standards of integrity with which all workers are expected to comply."[10] Clearly, American Standard believes in an external standard of conduct, or absolutes, that it expects everyone in the organization to practice.

External Sources

There are many examples of worldviews that derive their values from sources outside of man. Judaism and Islam are well-known examples. The former appeals to the Old Testament as its Bible and the latter to the Koran. Both of these worldviews embrace a set of absolutes to define values for the behavior of individuals and organizations. Neither seems to lead, however, to sustained prosperity. In his book, *Human Accomplishment,* agnostic researcher Charles Murray studied three thousand years of history and concluded that Christianity, or a biblical worldview, underlies virtually all human accomplishment.[11]

Christianity is an example of a worldview that recognizes an absolute source of authority outside of human beings, namely the Bible (both the Old and New Testament). It also recognizes that the Bible teaches that everyone has a conscience upon which God wrote the moral law. What God specifically delineated to the Jews in the Ten Commandments, He has implicitly written on the hearts of the Gentiles.[12]

A biblical worldview holds that the values revealed in the Bible are inherent in the heart of every person. It is these values that inform human beings that pride, murder, lying, coveting, adultery, and so forth, are wrong. Theologians generally refer to this level of revelation as "common grace," meaning that everyone, regardless of his or her worldview, has God's moral law written on his or her heart. This is why actions such as murder and stealing are universally regarded as wrong.

Notwithstanding the truth of common grace, a Christian or biblical worldview holds that the proper interpretation of the Bible requires a person to be regenerated and the Bible illuminated to that person by the Holy Spirit. This means that to move beyond the moral revelation of common grace, one must be born again and study the Bible under the illuminating work of the Holy Spirit.

A Biblical Worldview

To understand a biblical worldview, one must understand the story of the Bible. The Bible begins with the story of the origin of the universe. The first two chapters of the book of Genesis record this event. Part of the story is an explanation of why God made human beings. God made humans to rule His physical creation.[13] Ruling creation has two basic components—multiplying and subduing. To multiply means to increase, and "to subdue" means to understand and to master the God-ordained laws of the universe. Humans can only rule where they are physically present and understand how God designed things to work.

In the story of Creation in Genesis 1, there are several key principles of the universe that God reveals to us. One of these is the principle of species:

reproduction only occurs according to species. Humans can only reproduce humans. Plants can only reproduce plants. Animals can only reproduce animals. As simplistic as this sounds, it is important to understand that whatever is in the predecessor is in the successor.

The importance of the principle of species is clearly seen in the third chapter of Genesis, which records what theologians call "the Fall." Adam and Eve disobeyed a command of God—they sinned. This event complicated man's efforts to rule, because the sin of Adam and Eve, our ancestors, is passed on to every human being according to the principle of species.[14] There is now in the human race an irresistible propensity to sin.

Not only is the human race now impaired with a nature contrary to God, but the Bible states that the rest of creation is also impacted by sin.[15] Therefore man's ability to rule God's creation has been significantly impaired by sin.

Beginning with Genesis 3, the rest of the Bible is a record of God's heart to redeem man from sin and its consequences. The focal point of the story is the righteous requirement of God for sin: death. God's solution was to send His Son to die for the sin of mankind. According to the principle of species, God's Son, Jesus, would be of the same nature as God, which He was.[16] Through the death of Jesus, a new species was created—a species of the Spirit. Theologians use various terms to describe this species, such as, *born again, regenerated, redeemed,* and *justified.* This species has the ability to see the kingdom of God and to fulfill the divine design of man, to rule the universe.[17] The proper predicate for employing a biblical worldview to rule God's creation is being of the species of the Spirit.

The practical outworking of a biblical worldview is seen in the definition of success. Those who are not born of the Spirit denominate success in terms of money or prosperity, making money the goal of their work. Conversely, those who are of the species of the Spirit allow God to define success as alignment with Him.[18] Prosperity, as denominated in terms of financial and physical blessings, is the fruit of alignment with God. This distinction may seem subtle, but it is very significant. When money is the driving goal, people will compromise principles to attain the goal. God stated that principles, such as obedience, trump the sacrifice of ill-gotten assets.[19]

Though the Bible clearly teaches that the focus of the species of the Spirit is on obedience to God that leads to blessing, this does not eliminate trials and tribulation. Trials, tribulation, and struggle are used by God to refine us.[20] God's interest is in transforming the species of the Spirit into a people who look, in both theory and practice, like His Son.[21]

So why do wicked people prosper? The prophet Jeremiah mused over this question.[22] God's answer was that the prosperity of the wicked was only temporary.[23] Furthermore, the wicked are tools in God's hand to accomplish His purpose.[24] Long term, not being of the species of the Spirit will be fatal, even though there may be some temporary apparent success. Consider Enron, for example. This high-flying company came to an ignoble end when investors and lenders discovered the lies and deception that the company was cloaked behind.

A biblical worldview must also embrace the reality that God is incomprehensible and sovereign. Logically, one would expect that the Creator's nature would be far superior to that of His creatures, and it is.[25] A corollary is that His thinking processes are beyond ours.[26] Coupled to this is the reality that, as the Creator, He has the right to determine the course of events.[27] Therefore, it is logical that we would not be able to understand everything that God does and that God has the right to do as He pleases.[28] A biblical worldview must allow for the mystery of God that is rooted in His incomprehensibility and our finiteness. One of those mysteries is "common grace."

There are three types of people. First, there are those who are genuine members of the species of the Spirit as evidenced by the personal transformation in their lives. Second, there are those who profess to be of the species of the Spirit but display no evidence of the reality; hence, their condition or state is uncertain. They could be carnal Christians[29] or perhaps not Christians at all. In any case, there is little evidence of the transforming power of Christ in their lives. Third, there are those who make no claim to be of the species of the Spirit. These people clearly are not engaged in personal transformation.

Ideally, an organization would be composed of people who are of the species of the Spirit. These people are engaged in being transformed into the image of Christ and, therefore, walk according to a biblical worldview. Such people would walk not only in the principles of a biblical worldview, but also in the power of the Holy Spirit—a powerful combination rarely seen in most organizations, even churches. But the reality is that the workers in most organizations are not 100 percent of the species of the Spirit. But fret not— there is hope!

One of God's principles is that He blesses alignment with Him, even if people don't have a relationship with Him and are not of the species of the Spirit. This means that when people, either wittingly or unwittingly, obey God's principles they will be blessed. This is called "common grace."

Common grace is a term coined by theologians to describe God's favor and blessing generally and universally available to His created beings.[30] One aspect of His common grace is that He blesses those who humble themselves and honor Him. A good illustration of this is the centurion named Cornelius.[31] The Bible says that Cornelius was God-fearing and devout. He gave generously to those in need and prayed, but he didn't know the Lord. However, because of his humble attitude, God responded and sent a messenger to share the gospel of Jesus Christ. Obedience to God's principles, such as humility and generosity, led to blessings for Cornelius.

> WHEN PEOPLE, EITHER WITTINGLY OR UNWITTINGLY, OBEY GOD'S PRINCIPLES THEY WILL BE BLESSED. THIS IS CALLED "COMMON GRACE."

When people obey God's principles, such as the Golden Rule or counting the cost, there is blessing. This is common grace. Therefore, any organization can enjoy blessings from God simply by obeying any of His principles; however, the greatest level of blessing will be found by those organizations walking in a biblical worldview and in the power of the Holy Spirit.

Rejection of a Biblical Worldview

Rejection of a biblical worldview is fatal. Even though researchers have pragmatically discovered that the values and principles of a biblical worldview are at the root of sustained excellence in organizations, there are still many who don't understand this reality.

One of my former clients believed that good business meant never paying a bill until necessary. "Necessary" didn't mean when the bill was due, it meant when the vendor screamed. Furthermore, every bill was negotiable. His worldview, which was primarily based on the worship of money, was driven by the belief that he should hold on to money as long as he could. His Golden Rule was: "He who has the gold makes the rules." Because of this, he was continually disputing with creditors. Services were cut off. He was locked out of his office. The bank froze his accounts. The IRS came knocking. Despite all of this, he seemed to relish the challenge of working out of difficulty.

On the flip side, it was interesting to note what happened to this former client when someone owed him money. He was ruthless in doing whatever was necessary to collect. Because of his worldview, and therefore his life practices, he received numerous threats on his life and resorted to wearing a handgun on his belt. When I challenged his concept of the Golden Rule, my efforts were rebuffed. His value system, rooted in situational ethics (the end justifies the means), did not lead to sustained success. Living in lies and deception blesses no one. Ultimately, his clandestine business life led him to prison.

Rejection of biblical values and a biblical worldview is rejection of the God who created the universe. God's response to those that reject Him is to reject them.[32] Rejection by God is the ultimate punishment.

Dualism: The Enemy of a Biblical Worldview

If one has a biblical worldview, it is not surprising to discover that organizational excellence is rooted in compliance with the values and principles of the Bible. The Bible teaches many principles that we take for granted, such as, truth is better than lies, one reaps what one sows, lasting problem solving is based on dealing with root issues, and so on. The biblical book of Proverbs is full of truths that will facilitate success in any organization. Some have called Proverbs the handbook of business. Given that the Bible has so much information to help us with organizational success, why don't we avail ourselves of this treasure of truth? The answer is dualism.

Before R. G. (Bob) LeTourneau was a well-known designer and manufacturer of machines, he was a dualist.[33] His first venture into the business world was as an automobile mechanic. The effort was financially unsuccessful and Bob took a job moving dirt on a ranch. Since Bob was an honorable man, he intended to repay his debt from the failed business; the meager wages of his ranch job, however, made it a daunting task. He was overwhelmed with discouragement and his sister challenged him. She asked, "Don't you love our Savior?"[34] Surprised by the question, Bob answered yes and began to rattle off a list of activities that he and his wife did at church. Unimpressed, his sister pointed out that he did a lot of good deeds, but if he really loved Jesus, he would seek ways to serve Him. Going on, she noted that Bob was very dutiful, but he seemed to be only checking off a to-do list so that he could go back to work.

> SOME HAVE CALLED PROVERBS THE HANDBOOK OF BUSINESS.

Bob began an internal conversation with himself. He dismissed his sister's perspective; after all, she was a missionary and dealt with spiritual things. On the other hand, he was a dirt mover who dealt with physical things, and, therefore, not subject to her rules. However, in his heart he knew that he was wrong and she was right. He was dutiful, but not really honoring God.

The next Sunday at church, the pastor announced a week of revival meetings. Feeling spiritually bankrupt, Bob purposed to borrow the ranch vehicle to go. He went every night. The last night he waited until everyone was gone and then he went to the front of the church and fell on his knees in prayer. He asked the Lord to forgive him and he surrendered the rest of his life to the Lord's will. The glory of the Lord filled his soul. He knew that God had touched him.

Sleep was difficult that night as his heart raced with anticipation. What would the Lord want him to do? He believed that a businessman could never serve the Lord as a pastor or missionary could. Believing that his days as a businessman were over, Bob went to the pastor's home early the next morning to seek guidance on what the Lord would have him do.

The pastor received Bob warmly and invited him into his study. Bob recited his experience from the previous night to the pastor. He explained that he came to find out what God wanted him to do with the rest of his life. Wisely, the pastor invited Bob to pray with him. After their prayer, the pastor told Bob that "God needs businessmen as well as preachers and missionaries."[35]

This became a defining moment in Bob's life. Up to then Bob had been a dualist who believed that anyone who was really sold out to God had to be a preacher, missionary, pastor, or evangelist. But now he understood that being sold out to God was not about *what* one does, but about *how* one does it. In other words, work in virtually every field can be an expression of worship to God, if it is done with the right motives and principles.

GOD NEEDS BUSINESSMEN AS WELL AS PREACHERS AND MISSIONARIES.

This was a freeing revelation, because Bob loved to move dirt. He loved being outdoors, reshaping the earth, and bringing life to the desert by turning unproductive *terra firma* into fertile farm and ranch land. Now he could do what he had a passion to do and fulfill his commitment to God to dedicate the rest of his life to the Lord's service. Bob was free from dualism; he was free to glorify God with his work.

Dualism is the bifurcation of spiritual and material reality. It dates back over two thousand years to the early Greek philosophers who maintained that there were higher and lower planes of thought. The higher plane, known as *form*, contained universal truth and the lower plane, known as *substance*, contained temporal matter. The higher plane was viewed as superior to the temporal and imperfect world.

WORK IN VIRTUALLY EVERY FIELD CAN BE AN EXPRESSION OF WORSHIP.

It was an easy transition for the first-century Gnostics to extend the Greek thinking and assert that the physical world was inherently evil and the spiritual world good. Though the early church rejected the Gnostic belief, the medieval Catholic monks contributed to the propagation of dualism by hiring people to help them with the daily chores that they didn't have time to complete, such as tending gardens, milking cows, preparing meals, cleaning floors, making clothes, and doing laundry. The monks made it clear to the hired help, known as laymen, that spiritual activity was reserved for the monks.

Despite the Reformation's message that physical reality was important to God because God created the physical world and declared it to be good,[36] dualism didn't die. With time, it raised its head again in the protestant world and, as before, the perception was that material reality was inherently evil while spiritual reality was good.

Full Dualism

Today, dualism seems to have two forms—full dualism and partial dualism. Full dualism is generally embraced by non-Christians. It asserts that the Bible as taught by the church is irrelevant—that church, or religion, is a private matter that has varying degrees of relevancy to people, but it is largely not a factor in determining how people choose to live.

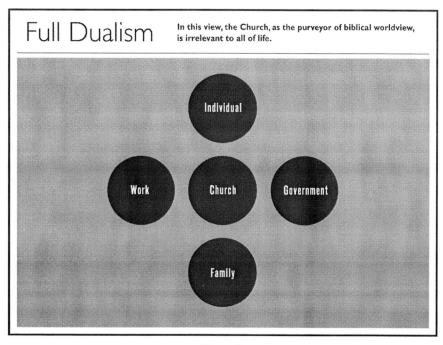

Diagram I

Diagram 1 shows five circles, each representing a sphere of authority that has been delegated by God to man. In the center of the diagram is the church. In a biblical worldview, the church defines truth and reality for all other spheres of authority.[37] Notice there is no connection between the church and any of the other jurisdictions. This symbolizes full dualism, which asserts that the church, the propagator of a biblical worldview, is irrelevant.

In the full dualistic model, the Bible and God are insignificant, since man develops his philosophy, principles, and values from some other source than the God of the Bible. This is the fullest expression of separation of church and state. It is separation of church from *everything*. It is easy to see examples of this model in society in the early part of the twenty-first century.

In the family jurisdiction, the long-held biblical definition of a family is under attack; homosexuals are seeking the right to marry. Civil government is systematically removing biblical symbols, such as the Ten Commandments, from public buildings—in the name of separation of church and state. Business is viewed as a secular activity. The mantra revealing the worldview of corporate America is "whatever works." Since the church is the purveyor of biblical worldview teaching, those who reject a biblical worldview reject the church as being relevant.

Partial Dualism

Partial dualism is very popular among Christians today because this view assumes that the God of the Bible is significant, at least for the individual and family. Diagram 2 illustrates partial dualism. Notice the arrows from the church to the individual and family. These arrows represent the authority that the church has to define the philosophy, principles, and values for these spheres of authority. There are no arrows from the church to work or government because, in this model, the church is not relevant to those spheres of authority.

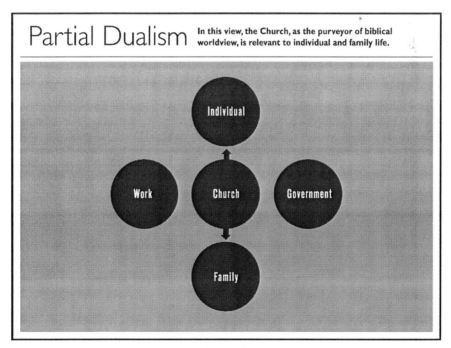

Diagram 2

As with the full dualism model, partial dualism embraces the doctrine of separation of church and state popular in the United States. Regrettably, proponents of this doctrine misunderstand the intent of our founding fathers. Rather than trying to protect the state from the church, they were trying to protect the church from the state. Having come from England where the church was controlled by the state, our ancestors were seeking to avoid the abuses they experienced in the motherland. The intent of the founding fathers was never to remove the influence of the church from the state. Instead, they looked to the Bible for guidance to govern the United States.

Not only is the separation of church and state commonly applied by many to civil government, but also to business, including education. The former president of Baylor University, a Baptist institution, asserted that religious faith has nothing to do with the pursuit of objective knowledge.[38] He also stated that religion is purely inward. In this view, religious convictions are private and therefore have no application outside the individual and family jurisdictions. Anyone holding this view would see the Bible, and therefore the church, as irrelevant outside of the personal and family spheres of authority.

The Integrated (Biblical) Worldview

The integration view holds that the Bible is the source of truth and reality for all the spheres of authority. This view is represented in Diagram 3.

Note the arrows from the church to each sphere of authority. These arrows mean that the philosophy, principles, and values for each sphere are rooted in the Bible. The Bible is the Creator's special revelation to His creation and is understood through the illuminating work of the Holy Spirit. The church's job is to teach biblical truth and thereby equip people to fulfill the individual purposes for which they were created.

God created the physical world and its values, and He expects us, His created beings, to rule His physical world. This mandate to rule encompasses all spheres of authority including government and business. In other words, the integrated model recognizes that God created the universe and, as the Creator, has every right to determine how every aspect of the universe is to be managed. Therefore, the philosophy, principles, and values for all of life are rooted in the Bible.

THE INTEGRATED MODEL RECOGNIZES THAT GOD CREATED THE UNIVERSE AND HAS EVERY RIGHT TO DETERMINE HOW EVERY ASPECT OF THE UNIVERSE IS TO BE MANAGED.

Regrettably few today, even among Christians, accept the integrated model. Most Christians are partial dualists. They maintain that God is not really interested in the physical world. Hence, God does not care how the physical world runs; therefore, the Bible does not contain much instruction as to how we are to govern ourselves and conduct business.

Perhaps unwittingly, some pastors and other "full-time" Christian workers promote the partial dualist point of view in the church. They do so when they suggest or imply that anyone who has an experience with God or who is truly serious about making his or her life count should go into "full-time Christian service." This presumes that the only valid callings of God are to "full-time ministry." Clearly, this perspective gives anyone working in the secular workplace a sense that they are second-class citizens. The sad reality is that second-class citizens do not effect change.

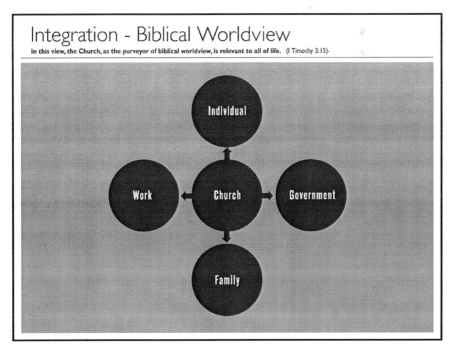

Integration - Biblical Worldview
In this view, the Church, as the purveyor of biblical worldview, is relevant to all of life. (I Timothy 3:15)-

Individual

Work   Church   Government

Family

Diagram 3

Ironically, many pastors muse over why their congregations are stagnant and ineffective. Could it be that the people don't feel that God cares about their secular work? Partial dualists think that God calls people to be missionaries, evangelists, and pastors, but that He never calls someone to be a businessman, tradesman, teacher, nurse, or politician; the value of anyone working in the secular workplace is only to make money to give to Christian causes and from time to time "preach the gospel and build up others in the faith."[39]

While these are certainly things that Christians should be doing, this partial dualistic perspective denies the dignity and value of work in the physical world. Furthermore, it denies the relevancy of the Bible in providing the philosophy, values, and principles needed to manage organizations.

If one believes the Bible in Genesis 1:26–28, man was created by God to rule the physical world. Ruling meant two things: multiplying and subduing. Furthermore, God repeatedly declared that the physical world was "good."[40] If God values the physical world by calling it good, shouldn't we value it as well? Should we not also expect that God would reveal the philosophy, values, and principles in the Bible that He wants humans to use to manage the physical world that He created?

EVERYONE'S WORK IS IMPORTANT TO GOD.

By embracing the value of both spiritual and physical work, one obtains a worldview that values and integrates both spiritual and physical reality. This integrated perspective seems to be more consistent with biblical teaching. In this view, everyone is created for a purpose and everyone's work is important to God.

This reality empowers people, who seek out the reason for their being, to be change agents wherever they are called to work because they know their contribution is significant. Even non-Christians, such as Charles Murray, recognize that human achievement occurs when people feel that they are created for a purpose, that the major reason for life is to fulfill that purpose, and that their work counts.[41]

The integrated view recognizes and values the calling of all believers. There are no second-class citizens in the kingdom of God. Everyone has a purpose. Everyone's work counts. Dennis Peacocke captured this concept well when he said: "There is a spiritual revolution in the making, one like unto Martin Luther's 'priesthood of all believers' revolution. Not only are all believers priests before the Lord, as Luther maintained, but all Spirit-directed vocations are ordained by God and intrinsically of value."[42]

> **"ALL SPIRIT-DIRECTED VOCATIONS ARE ORDAINED BY GOD AND INTRINSICALLY OF VALUE."**
> **– DENNIS PEACOCKE**

This book assumes that the integrated model is the correct approach to defining the philosophy, principles, and values for every sphere of authority. The rationale for the integrated model is simple: if God made the universe and commissioned man to rule in certain spheres of authority, then it follows that He made the rules for mankind to rule the various spheres. His rules (philosophy, values, and principles) are found by alignment with His view of reality, which is known as a biblical worldview.

The Superiority of a Biblical Worldview

The previous discussion is based on several important assumptions. First, I assumed that God exists and has revealed Himself to His creation. Second, I assumed that God has revealed Himself through the Bible as His inspired and inerrant Word. Third, I assumed that we humans have the ability to understand God's revelation.

God's revelation is twofold. First, there is revelation in creation, which theologians call "general revelation." General revelation is revelation available to everyone. It is the revelation of divine design in nature[43] that testifies to the existence of a creator. (Note that creation points to the existence of a creator but does not prove it.) Second, the Bible is referred to as "special revelation" in that it is God's special revelation about His redemptive work through His Son, Jesus Christ. The Bible teaches that its message must be discerned spiritually to correctly interpret it; therefore, a person must receive the illumination of the Holy Spirit.[44]

Given that everyone is a person of faith, meaning that we all live based on presuppositions or beliefs, and if you accept my basic presuppositions, the logic for a biblical worldview as the foundation for organizational excellence seems compelling. If God created the universe He makes the rules of the games that the created beings are to play. God created the laws of physics that govern the universe; He also created the laws that govern business, government, and social behavior. Why would anyone think that there are laws that govern organizational practice that exist apart from the Creator of the universe?

Consider also that of all the countries in the world, the United States is arguably the one rooted most clearly in a biblical worldview. The founding fathers were known for their Christian perspective. By some accounts, the majority of the population of the United States claims to be Christian. Now note that the United States is the leader in technology innovation and could colonize the world, but chooses not to. It also serves as the leader in policing the world and provides aid for the whole world. Furthermore, it is a world leader in GDP/capita/year at $37.5K.[45] Catholic Spain's GDP/capita/year is $17.5K.[46] The Muslim Arab nations' GDP/capita/year is $1.9K.[47] And India, which is largely Hindu, enjoys a GDP/capita/year of $480.[48]

The amazing reality is that even though the United States is trying to divorce itself from a biblical worldview, it still enjoys the fruit of faithfulness to the biblical worldview of its founding fathers. If indeed biblical worldview is the foundation for national blessings, it should also be the foundation for organizational blessings.

The organization that understands this principle is rare; many embrace elements of a biblical worldview without realizing it. Consider for example companies such as American Standard, Boeing, and Dow Chemical.

The *Code of Conduct and Ethics* of American Standard states: "These standards are not voluntary. They are mandatory. They flow from laws that control our conduct around the world and from values that define who we are as a company."[49] The reference to "laws that control our conduct around the world" is an unwitting reference to the universal reality of biblical principles and values. Where else would these laws come from? The fact that American Standard expects every employee, officer, director, and vendor to comply[50] with the *Code of Conduct and Ethics* implies a belief in absolute principles and values that transcend individuals and cultures.

Boeing's Web site states: "Ethics is deeply ingrained in our culture. Strong commitments to integrity, fairness, quality, and excellence have long been guiding principles."[51] Where would one go to find the origin of these values? There can be little doubt that the values embraced find their roots in the Bible, and hence, in a biblical view of reality.

Bill Stavropoulos, chairman, president, and CEO of Dow Chemical Company, stated: "An honest, transparent, and trustworthy corporate culture bolsters employee morale, builds customer trust, and ultimately guards stockholder value. Simply stated, good governance and ethics are not only the right thing to do, they make for good business."[52] Mr. Stravropoulos clearly recognizes the value of honesty, transparency, and trust. He believes that embracing these values is "right," and that doing so will lead to good results. As with American Standard and Boeing, Dow Chemical unabashedly builds on biblical values and principles.

Every organization must adopt a philosophy and corresponding principles and values that define its culture and methods of operation. Enduring excellent organizations are organizations whose foundations are rooted, either wittingly or unwittingly, in a biblical worldview. The rationale for such an approach is simple: if the God of the Bible created the universe, He created the rules of the universe. Therefore, if one believes in the God of the Bible, one must look to the Bible to provide the rules by which individuals and organizations were designed to function.

This reality is easily validated by the observation of the philosophy, principles, and values adopted by successful, enduring organizations. Philosophically, great organizations recognize that the reason for their existence is far beyond making money. These organizations have a sense of societal purpose and significance. Consistently, successful organizations articulate a strong and clear commitment to integrity, honesty, trust, service, and excellence—all of which are biblical values.

> **THE PRINCIPLES OF ORGANIZATIONAL EXCELLENCE CANNOT BE SEPARATED FROM THE BIBLE.**

In addition, principles such as the Golden Rule are eagerly embraced to define standards of conduct for dealing with workers, customers, vendors, regulators, and so on. Contrary to the thinking of many, the principles of organizational excellence and prosperity cannot be separated from the Bible. If the Creator of the universe reveal His principles in the Bible, we, God's created beings, must pay heed. Utilizing biblical values and principles is the only way to build great and lasting organizations.

Conclusion

Worldview is the conceptual basis upon which every organization is built. The collective behavior of an organization is a direct reflection of its worldview and the ability of the organization to express its worldview consistently. If one believes that the God of the Bible created the universe, it follows that the same God made the rules for our personal life, family life, church life, business life, and community life.

I believe that the God of Christianity is the only true God and that He has made the rules of the organizational behavior game. Anyone wishing to prosper must align with God's philosophy, principles, and values (the rules of the game). The God of Christianity blesses alignment with Himself and opposes those who oppose Him.[53] The rest of this book is about applying a biblical worldview to organizational behavior. The goal is to achieve excellence.[54] After all, He created the universe and therefore owns it; we are all His stewards. So let's be about playing the game—by His rules.

Points to Ponder

1. What are the key presuppositions that undergird your worldview?

2. What are the key presuppositions that undergird the worldview of your organization?

3. Why is humanism commonly rejected by organizations but widely embraced by individuals?

4. Are you living dualistically? Defend your answer with examples from your life (i.e., choices, priorities, attitudes).

5. How have you integrated a biblical worldview into your personal, family, church, business, and community life?

Notes

1. http://www.inspirelist.com, September 12, 2003.

2. See Jeremiah 17:9.

3. Constance L. Hays, "Social Issues Tug Wal-Mart in Different Directions," *New York Times*, 30 June 2004.

4. Kevin and Jackie Freiberg, *Nuts* (Bard Press, 1996), chapter 6.

5. *World Magazine*, 26 July 2003.

6. Jim Collins and Jerry Porras, *Built to Last* (NY: HarperBusiness, 1997), II.

7. Leonard Berry, *Discovering the Soul of Service* (NY: The Free Press, 1999), 236.

8. Collins and Porras, *Built to Last,* 221.

9. John D. Beckett, *Loving Monday* (Downers Grove, IL: InterVarsity Press, 1998, 2001), 66.

10. http://www.americanstandard.com/conduct.asp (as of September 24, 2003).

11. Susan Olasky, "Gaining Ground," *World*, 10 January 2004.

12. Romans 2:14–15.

13. Genesis 1:26–28.

14. 1 Corinthians 15:22.

15. Genesis 3:17, Romans 8:22.

16. Philippians 2:5–6.

17. John 3.

18. Deuteronomy 30:16–20.

19. 2 Samuel 15:22.

20. James 1:2ff.

21. Romans 8:29.

22. Jeremiah 12:1.

23. Jeremiah 12:14–17.

24. Proverbs 16:4.

25. Exodus 15:11.

26. Isaiah 55:8.

27. Isaiah 46:9–11.

28. Romans 9:19–20.

29. I Corinthians 3:3.

30. Matthew 5:45.

31. Acts 10.

32. Deuteronomy 31:1–22.

33. R. G. LeTourneau, *R.G. LeTourneau: Mover of Men and Mountains* (Chicago: Moody Press, 1967), 107–110.

34. Ibid., 107.

35. Ibid., 109.

36. Genesis 1.

37. 1 Timothy 3:15.

38. Gene Edward Veith, "Baptist Brawl," *World,* 14 February 2004.

39. Tommy Ice in the "The End of the World," *Business Reform*, vol. 3, no. 2, 8.

40. Genesis 1.

41. Susan Olasky, "Gaining Ground," *World*, 10 January 2004.

42. Dennis Peacocke, *Doing Business God's Way* (Rebuild, 2003), 6–7.

43. Romans 1:18–32.

44. 1 Corinthians 2.

45. *Wall Street Journal,* March 2003.

46. W*orld Magazine*, 29 March 2003, 20ff.

47. Ibid.

48. Amy Waldman, "Sizzling Economy Revitalizes India," *New York Times*, 20 October 2003.

49. American Standard Companies, *Our Code of Conduct and Ethics*, 5.

50. Ibid.

51. http://www.boeing.com/companyoffices/aboutus/ethics/index.htm as of September 24, 2003.

52. *PR Newswire,* 17 July 2003.

53. Proverbs 3:33.

54. Colossians 3:23.

Beyond Babel Model

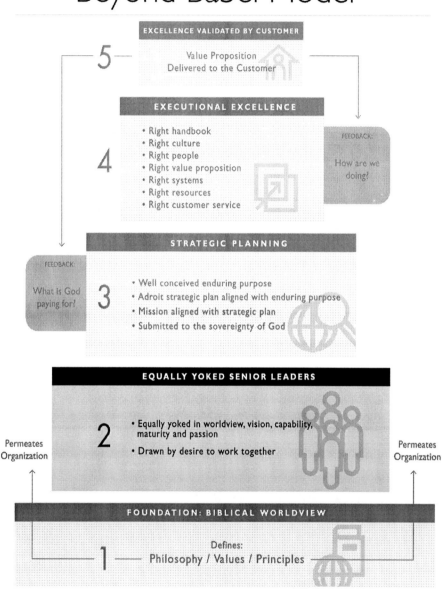

EXCELLENCE VALIDATED BY CUSTOMER

5 · · · · Value Proposition
Delivered to the Customer

EXECUTIONAL EXCELLENCE

4
- Right handbook
- Right culture
- Right people
- Right value proposition
- Right systems
- Right resources
- Right customer service

FEEDBACK:

How are we doing?

STRATEGIC PLANNING

FEEDBACK:

What is God paying for?

3
- Well conceived enduring purpose
- Adroit strategic plan aligned with enduring purpose
- Mission aligned with strategic plan
- Submitted to the sovereignty of God

EQUALLY YOKED SENIOR LEADERS

2
- Equally yoked in worldview, vision, capability, maturity and passion
- Drawn by desire to work together

Permeates Organization

Permeates Organization

FOUNDATION: BIBLICAL WORLDVIEW

1 —— Defines:
Philosophy / Values / Principles

Equally Yoked
Senior Leaders

How good and pleasant it is
when brothers live together in unity!
It is like precious oil poured on the head,
running down on the beard,
running down on Aaron's beard,
down upon the collar of his robes.
It is as if the dew of Hermon
were falling on Mount Zion.
For there the LORD *bestows his blessing,*
even life forevermore.[1]

Do two walk together unless they have agreed to do so?[2]

If a house is divided against itself, that house cannot stand.[3]

The Importance of Unity

Unity is indeed sweet. It is characterized by harmony, love, forbearance, and acceptance. Disunity is characterized by strife, hatred, and conflict. Unity enables and facilitates people to accomplish great feats. Disunity is disruptive and chaotic. Who wants disunity? Everyone wants an environment where he or she can enjoy unity. Whether family, business, church, or government, everyone wants to enjoy the fruits of unity.

To achieve a high level of excellence, an organization must have unified leadership. This principle may seem quite trivial, but its reality is powerful. As an illustration, consider World War II. That war was fought on fronts spanning the globe against three very formidable enemies—Germany, Japan, and Italy. At the beginning of the war, Germany had a clear advantage in military technology. Despite the expanse of the war and the initial technical disadvantage, the United States and its allies won a resounding victory. The opposite was true of the Vietnam War. This war was fought against one opponent in a localized setting where America had a clear technological advantage, yet America lost.

How is it that the United States could win a global war so decisively yet lose so miserably in Vietnam? The difference was unity. In World War II, there was no doubt that the United States had to fight this war and Americans made the sacrifices needed to win. The unity was enormous. However, in Vietnam, America was greatly divided over whether or not it should be conducting this war. Such division led to internal conflict and strife, diverting focus and energy away from the task of winning the war. As a result, America lost the war.

UNITY IS THE KEY TO ACCOMPLISHING GREAT FEATS.

Unity is the key to accomplishing great feats regardless of the venue—the family, business, government, the church, an educational institution, or a nonprofit. Unified leadership is a fundamental and critical building block of excellence. Unity in any organization begins at the top with the leaders and then flows throughout the organization. If the leaders are not unified, the organization will not be unified, and excellence is compromised.

The rest of this chapter articulates the key characteristics of unified senior leadership that facilitate organizational excellence.

The Concept of Equal Yoking

*Do not be yoked together with unbelievers. For what do righ-
teousness and wickedness have in common? Or what fellow-
ship can light have with darkness? What harmony is there
between Christ and Belial? What does a believer have in
common with an unbeliever? What agreement is there between the temple of God and idols? For we are the temple of
the living God. As God has said: "I will live with them and
walk among them, and I will be their God, and they will be
my people."*[4]

Most people who have been exposed to the Bible for any length of time
have heard a message on these verses. This text is rooted in Isaiah 52:1–14,
which speaks of Israel's ultimate redemption from captivity and the deliverance
of Jerusalem from the defilement of her captors. Of course, the captivity was
judgment upon Israel for rebellion.

In the New Testament epistle to the church at Corinth, the apostle Paul
uses this text[5] to defend his ministry and encourage the Corinthian church to
not be influenced by worldviews contrary to a Christian perspective.

The reality of yoking is easy to see in marriage, but yoking happens in all of life.
Yoking occurs anytime two or more people unite to accomplish a common goal or mission. People
who accept Christ as their Savior are yoked to Him to accomplish His purposes. When a person
accepts a job with an organization, the person is yoked to the organization and should support the
mission and goals of the organization. By joining a church, a person is yoked with the other members of the church and should
reflect the worldview represented by the church. Whatever community you
live in, you are yoked to that community and should be working for the
common good of the community.

> **YOKING OCCURS ANYTIME TWO OR MORE PEOPLE UNITE TO ACCOMPLISH A COMMON GOAL.**

The metaphor to convey the principle of yoking is a farming motif
common in the first-century agrarian society. When plowing ground, a farmer

would frequently want more power than one animal could provide, so he would yoke two together, generally in parallel. (For these discussions, parallel yoking is assumed.) The presupposition of the farmer was that the two animals were of equal capability, as the combined force vector of the two animals was clearly more powerful than the force of one.

The assumption of equal capability means animals would be the same type. Furthermore, the animals would be comparable in maturity, strength, health, and motivation. If any of these characteristics were not true, one of the animals would perform with more force than the other. When two animals are yoked together, a system is formed consisting of the animals and the physical yoke. The system has a center of mass somewhere between the two animals. The net force vector of the work of the two animals can be viewed as emanating from the center of mass. Though the animal's individual force vectors are parallel, the vectors are not co-located. Therefore, there is a component of each animal's force vector that is perpendicular to the net force vector. This means that there is some inefficiency in even the most perfectly or equally yoked systems. The inefficiency is associated with the force required to keep the yoked system in balance. The net result is a system moving straight, along the line of the net force vector acting on the center of mass and held in balance by the perpendicular balancing force.

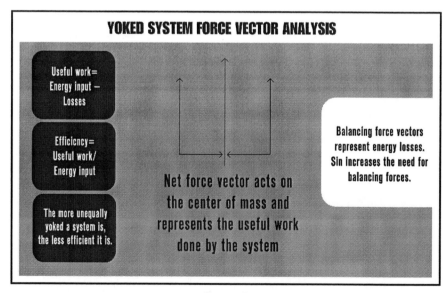

YOKED SYSTEM FORCE VECTOR ANALYSIS

Useful work=
Energy input –
Losses

Efficiency=
Useful work/
Energy input

The more unequally
yoked a system is,
the less efficient it is.

Net force vector acts on
the center of mass and
represents the useful work
done by the system

Balancing force vectors
represent energy losses.
Sin increases the need for
balancing forces.

Diagram 4

Diagram 4 illustrates the vectors involved in a yoked system with two sources of energy, such as two people working together to accomplish a common goal. Clearly, the objective is to convert as much energy as possible to useful work. The degree of unequal yoking defines the amount of balancing energy required. The less balancing energy required, the more useful work is produced. An example of unequal yoking is any sin operative in one or both of the sources of energy.

Given that the best of yoked systems is not perfect, what happens when the animals are not of equal capability? Remember, the assumption is that the best of yoked systems has animals of equal type, maturity, strength, health, and motivation. If there is inequality in any of these areas, then the perpendicular force vectors are not balanced. The result is that the system no longer moves in a straight line without compensation from the stronger animal. This reduces the amount of energy available to move the system in a straight line. Efficiency is the ratio of useful work performed divided by the total work. Though perpendicular forces are necessary to maintain system balance, they do not contribute to the objective of pulling the plow in a straight line. Therefore, the balancing force is inversely proportional to the efficiency of the system.

So how does this metaphor apply in other areas of life? Many who are familiar with the Christian faith readily apply it to marriage. Hitler applied it illicitly to ethnic purity, which is one of the reasons that he sought to exterminate the Jews. Others extend the application to churches. The Plymouth Brethren are one such example who embraced this reality. Some paradigms of this movement are called "exclusive brethren" because they excluded anyone that they deemed was not equally yoked with them. But does this principle of equal yoking apply to work in the modern workplace?

THE DEGREE THAT THE YOKING IS EQUAL, IS A MEASURE OF THE EFFICIENCY OF THE ORGANIZATION.

Let's talk about work in terms of organizational behavior. After all, organizations are simply groups of people who have come together to accomplish a mission. In this context, is equal yoking important? Clearly, if you want to win a military battle, it is vital that all of your resources work together. If you want an effective institution of education, the various grade levels need to be synchronized. If you want efficiency in a manufacturing plant, the processes need to be coordinated and arranged in the proper sequence. These are examples of yoking. The degree that the yoking is equal is a measure of the efficiency of the organization.

Unequal Yoking

> *They [Israelites; see Numbers 25] yoked themselves to the Baal of Peor [took on a false worldview] and ate sacrifices offered to lifeless gods.*[6]

Everyone is a person of faith. Everyone makes assumptions about truth that form the foundation of a belief system out of which one's worldview emanates. All of one's behavior is a direct reflection and consequence of one's worldview, because everyone is irresistibly yoked to his or her worldview.

When one fails to embrace a biblical worldview, one is yoked to an idol. Being yoked to idols in the workplace is inefficient. A good example of this is the worship of cattle in India. I am told that when a cow enters a road, all cars stop until the cow moves. Likewise if a cow wanders onto a railroad track or an airport runway, the trains and airplanes stop until the cow leaves. Cow manure is considered sacred and therefore is not removed from public places. I think it is abundantly clear that this worldview promotes neither efficient work nor public health.

Perhaps a more relevant example is that of WorldCom in the early part of the twenty-first century. WorldCom was a high-flying company that was caught up in the worship of money. As a result, values such as honesty were compromised for the sake of producing the illusion of growing quarterly profits. Growing profits pleased Wall Street; however, investors didn't wish to be deceived. In the end, when the truth came out, the financial world revealed its angst for the lies and deception of WorldCom. WorldCom became unequally yoked with its investors and lenders. The end result was bankruptcy for WorldCom.

Inefficiencies and conflict occur when a person's worldview is at odds with the worldview of a business partner. This unequal yoking can show up as a conflict in vision, strategy, values, and/or operating principles. This is what happened to my dad with his first business partner. Similarly unequal yoking can occur between a subordinate and superior, particularly if the superior is expecting behavior that the subordinate believes compromises his or her worldview.

On more than one occasion, I have seen managers impose their will on a subordinate who felt intimidated and coerced into capitulating to the perspective of, and actions desired by the manager. The culture of an organization can create conflict when expectations of behavior conflict with the worldview of workers. On one occasion, a client told me that one of his administrative assistants was conflicted when a salesperson submitted for reimbursement for inappropriately entertaining a customer.

Conflicts between the worldview of customers and organizations occur when customers fail to pay, expect kickbacks, or engage in bid shopping. The reverse is also true. Organizations may fail to deliver products and/or services with excellence and integrity, which leads to conflict with customers. Mutual fund investors can be unequally yoked with others because different investors may have different worldviews. When fear drives some to sell, this can impact the others as fund managers may be forced to liquidate investment positions at inopportune times. Civil authorities who engage in bribery and injustice will be at odds with those whose worldview embraces honesty and justice.

Unequal yoking at work, in government, at school, in families, or in churches inevitably leads to conflict. Conflict drains people and organizations of resources that could be more efficiently used to produce quality products and services. Unequal yoking of worldviews robs people and organizations of the necessary alignment to operate at peak efficiency.

Equal Yoking

> *At that time Jesus said, "I praise you, Father, Lord of heaven and earth, because you have hidden these things from the wise and learned, and revealed them to little children. Yes, Father, for this was your good pleasure.*
>
> *"All things have been committed to me by my Father. No one knows the Son except the Father, and no one knows the*

Father except the Son and those to whom the Son chooses to reveal him.

"Come to me, all you who are weary and burdened, and I will give you rest. Take my yoke upon you and learn from me, for I am gentle and humble in heart, and you will find rest for your souls. For my yoke is easy and my burden is light." [7]

This text gives us a clue as to what is meant by equal yoking. Equal yoking comes from walking in a continuous process of revelation from the Son of God. The revelation is about God the Father whom only God the Son knows. The Son graciously imparts the knowledge of the Father to those whom He chooses. Knowing the Father is about gaining His perspective, embracing His values, walking in His principles, and learning His ways. (This is another way of saying biblical worldview.) The fruit of this impartation is revelation that brings rest to our souls.

Most people enjoy the unity, peace, and productivity that is the result of being equally yoked. This reality is the pinnacle of organizational efficiency and excellence. An organization functioning at this level experiences incredible favor. The people in the organization find great satisfaction in their work and are therefore highly motivated. The customers and clients value the organization and gladly pay a premium for the products and services. Vendors and regulators find these organizations a joy, not a burden.

Equal yoking facilitates the impartation of wisdom from the Father through the Son of God. The reason any organization exists is to solve problems. The solution to any problem is the same—wisdom. The source of all wisdom is the Creator of the universe who makes all the rules for all the games. Therefore, for any organization to truly prosper, there must be equal yoking to facilitate the flow of impartation from the Son to the organization. Unequal yoking blocks the flow of wisdom to an organization, which impairs the organization's ability to efficiently produce excellent products and services.

The Bible records the story of the Tower of Babel.[8] As people were populating the earth, the text states that a number of them moved eastward and settled in a plain called Shinar. They desired to build a city with a tower that reached to the heavens. The tower was to be a landmark and symbol of unity because the people desired to make a name for themselves. The Lord viewed it as a presage to more self-exalting behavior and brought judgment on them by disrupting their command and control. This story illustrates the power of unity, focus, technology, and communication, and also the judgment of God upon projects and organizations that pursue projects with the wrong motives.

The people were unified in their desire to elevate themselves, so they yoked themselves together. Using the best technology of the day (uniformly shaped bricks instead of irregularly shaped stones), they submitted themselves to each other to accomplish the task. The project was illicit because it lacked the proper motive. Therefore, divine intervention disrupted the communication bringing the project to a stop. Despite the illicit purpose of the project, this incident shows the power of equal yoking.

Regardless of the motives, when people are equally yoked there is great power to accomplish tasks—temporarily. They had a common worldview built around self-exaltation and a common purpose to build the city with the tower. Success would have been theirs were it not for the judgment of God because of their heart to self-exalt.

Yoking yourself with others is an act of humility, submission, and teamwork. Though the people building the Tower of Babel wanted to make a name for themselves, they had to subordinate their individual agendas to the agenda of the whole. Hence, there was submission to one another and a willingness to work as a team. The common good was the overriding goal to which everyone submitted.

Even though the people who built the Tower of Babel were not fully aligned with the Creator, they were partially aligned. They embraced many of His values. This is the only reason that they enjoyed success. If partial alignment brings blessings, how much more blessing will one receive by fully aligning with God's philosophy, values, and principles?

Yoking Challenges

There are many different ways that we are yoked to others. Every organization and relationship is a yoking situation—families, companies, churches, investment clubs, and so forth. Any time one joins with others to accomplish something, one is yoked with people. To maximize one's opportunity for success, one must seek to be equally yoked.

Consider the following examples of yoking:

Different types of animals

This represents different worldviews. The Bible states that an ox and a donkey should not be yoked together.[9] The reason is that they are very different in their basic capabilities. The difference in physical capability is comparable to differences in worldview. Differences in worldview lead to differences in values, principles, priorities, and goals.

Consider an experience of one of the sales engineers who worked for me in the family business. He walked into my office one day to announce, with glee, that he sold a job and the customer told him that price was not a concern. I immediately knew what the customer meant. The customer didn't intend to pay. Why was this unequal yoking? The reason was simple. My family business promptly paid its vendors. This customer's worldview, however, was totally different from ours. His concept of good business was to avoid paying unless he was forced to pay. This difference in worldview created unequal yoking and the corresponding conflict.

Same type of animals

This represents worldview alignment. The same type of animals should have similar capabilities. In reality, however, there are numerous ways that animals of the same species can be different—age, health, motivation, and maturity. The same type of animal represents worldview alignment in theory. Consider, however, the following examples of unequal yoking between the same type of animals.

- Within any species of animals there can be differences in capabilities in size, weight, and strength. This is analogous to different gifts and abilities. The experience of one of my clients illustrates what happens when unequal yoking occurs.

A family business was passed on to the next generation when the founder retired. His son and daughter took over the management of the company. Production management, which was the purview of the founder, was left in the hands of a less than competent but loyal company man. This led to unequal yoking that persisted for several years. Year after year, production failed to meet expectations. Everyone on the team was able to pull his or her weight except the production manager. During this time, the company floundered. Production was slow and profits were nil. Finally the production manager was replaced with a competent individual who enabled the company to dramatically move forward. Within a few months, production was dramatically improved and profits soared. For this company, this experience of unequal yoking was the difference between profit and loss.

* Another example of unequal yoking with the same type of animal is age. Older animals do not have the strength and stamina of younger ones, but the older animals possess wily skill. More than once, I have encountered young eager entrepreneurs with more zeal than wisdom.

I have a standard speech ready for these encounters when I am asked my opinion about starting a business. The speech is a short monologue stating that *it will be harder than you think, take longer than you think, and cost more than you think.* The usual response is stunned chagrin, which means that the entrepreneurs typically press forward despite the well-known statistic that 80 percent of all business startups fail within the first five years.[10] Unequal yoking happens when these young entrepreneurs, operating more out of zeal than wisdom, start businesses with capital from investors who are expecting the entrepreneurs to act based on wisdom rather than zeal.

* Health, physical and/or emotional, is another factor in yoking. When anyone is severely ill physically, work becomes difficult. Likewise, anyone with personal problems will have difficultly focusing on work.

A construction company enjoyed an outstanding reputation and was highly successful. This company operated with impeccable values and principles. The owner, who was a key member of the senior management team, became involved with the company secretary. He divorced his wife of more than thirty years to marry his young secretary. Soon afterward, he knew that he had made a big mistake and went into a prolonged depression. As a result, his performance dropped and his company started a long slide downhill from which the company never fully recovered. He became unequally yoked to the team and the other members of the team could not compensate for his poor performance. As a result, the company went into a decline that was nearly irreversible.

- Motivation is a big factor with everyone. When someone has a passion to do something, nothing will stop him or her. In fact, Jim Collins asserts that the whole concept of motivating workers is false. He argues that everyone has a passion to do something. Therefore the role of management is to help people find their passion and then get out of their way.[11]

One of my clients had an eye-opening experience when he discovered that his management team did not share his passion for working with excellence. Though my client was the sole owner, he expected his management team to work as he did and go the extra mile to be sure everything was done properly. He was disabused of his perspective as he observed that they were more concerned about weekends than work. Though his management team was competent, my client's ability to grow his business was severely impaired because he was not equally yoked motivationally with his team. Jim Collins would assert that my client didn't have the right people on the bus or didn't have the right compensation package in place.[12]

It is important to understand that equal yoking does not preclude diversity. Diversity is a powerful reality in the context of equal yoking. For example, the basic functions of any organization are to get work, do work, and keep score. Each of these functions requires different capabilities. For an organization to operate efficiently, however, each function requires a leader that can work in harmony with the other team members.

Hopefully you can see the power of being equally yoked and the penalty for being unequally yoked. With equal yoking there is peace and prosperity. With unequal yoking there is conflict, inefficiency, and loss. Who wants the fruit of unequal yoking? I trust, no one. So how does one find an organization with which one can experience equal yoking? The answer is C4.

The Power of C4

When I worked in the family business, it was my practice to walk around the building at least once every day. Some people refer to this as "management by walking around." My daily stroll took me through every department, including the sheet metal shop. The sheet metal shop was staffed with six to twelve people, depending on the workload, and was tasked with making ductwork and other metal products needed to install mechanical systems in buildings. Frequently, fiberglass insulation was attached to the inside of the metal duct for acoustical and thermal purposes. The task of attaching this material was not easy, because of the nature of fiberglass; most people in the shop tried to avoid it. However, there was one man who consistently performed this task. Not only did he do the task, he worked hard and was highly productive.

It is wise for a boss not to question why someone is working so hard. My curiosity, however, was getting the best of me, so I asked. His answer was quite interesting. He said, "I love what I do." I thought, *Wow, someone loves to do the dirty job of attaching fiberglass onto sheet metal. What a marvelous reality! He loves his work and therefore is very productive.* Then I looked around at others in the shop and began to realize that they were not nearly as productive in what they did, even though they were doing tasks that were not nearly as messy and dirty. Could the reason be that they didn't love their work?

As simplistic as this observation was, it launched me into the search for what drives people to be excellent workers. As a business consultant, I have worked with dozens of companies in a wide variety of industries. My experience is that few people are highly productive at work. Why is this?

Consider the hypothesis that most people have not found the right job. If most people found the right job, one would expect highly motivated, and therefore, productive workers. Of course, this assumes that there is a right job for each person. To believe that there is a right job for each human being implies that there is intelligent design in creation. That is, each person is created for a reason. Also, the gifting and calling of each person are congruent.

Furthermore, if there is intelligent design, one would expect that it is incumbent on each created being to discover his or her reason for being and to pursue it.

> **FEW PEOPLE ARE HIGHLY PRODUCTIVE AT WORK.**

My assumption is that every person is created for a purpose. It doesn't matter what kind of work one does—janitor, salesperson, secretary, executive, professional, middle manager, blue-collar worker, cook, homemaker, and so forth. Every person has value by virtue of being created by God. And God is about executing His purpose in the universe.[13] That being the case, my thesis is that if a person discovers the reason for his or her existence and commits to fulfilling his or her destiny, then that person will do excellent work.

> **MOST PEOPLE HAVE NOT FOUND THE RIGHT JOB.**

If this is true, how do we recognize someone who is walking in his or her destiny? Or stated another way, is there a set of characteristics that enables a person to discover his or her ideal job—the place where he or she can excel and be highly productive? I submit to you that there are four key characteristics, which I call C4: calling, character, capability, and commissioning. The best person to perform any job is someone with C4 to do that job. A person's destiny is defined as the work for which that the person possesses C4.

Calling

Calling is an issue of the heart; it is a measure of passion. Passion is what drives people to find out what they are supposed to do in life. It is the internal quality that makes one restless and yearn to find fulfillment and satisfaction in life. Jesus expressed this quality when He said, *"I must be about my Father's business.* "[14] Nehemiah possessed this quality as he prepared to rebuild Jerusalem after the judgment on the Jewish people for not obeying the Lord.[15] When Moses was building the tabernacle, he sought people whose *"heart is stirred"*[16] to do the work. For my sheet metal worker previously mentioned, there was no question that he had a strong passion to do what he was doing. He reflected that in his attitude and his hard work.

A Ph.D. chemist sought counsel from me relative to his job. He had been hired by a medical school to maintain the technical equipment of the research laboratory. A few years after joining the school, he was promoted to assistant professor, which meant that he could now seek grant money to do research. The problem was that he didn't know what to pursue. He was so lost that he spent his spare time reading the news rather than working on grant proposals. I asked him what was in his heart. He

> **IF A PERSON DISCOVERS THE REASON FOR HIS OR HER EXISTENCE AND COMMITS TO FULFILLING HIS OR HER DESTINY, THEN THAT PERSON WILL DO EXCELLENT WORK.**

said that he loved NMR (nuclear magnetic resonance) work and had pursued a Ph.D. to do this type of work. He cited a situation where he was asked to analyze a substance. Quickly he realized that NMR was the best tool to perform this analysis. The thrill of using NMR to solve this problem was so great that he stayed up late and solved the problem before morning. The next day he went back into his funk because he could not see a research project to do that would use NMR. This is a wonderful picture of what happens to all of us. When we do what we were created to do, the passion is enormous.

Calling is the most fundamental of all qualities that anyone should look for in hiring a person or finding a job. Without heart, people cannot have passion. And without passion, people cannot work enduringly and productively with excellence.

Character

Some years ago, Henry Ford lamented, "Why is it that I always get the whole person, when what I really want is a pair of hands?"[17] Mr. Ford was dealing with the reality that when he hired anyone, he hired the person's worldview and, consequently, the person's value system. There is no way to separate a person's skill from a person's character. Character is an integral part of every person and is the root driver of most of the decisions that people make. Character is an expression of our beliefs and values, and is the basis for our life choices.

For example, the Japanese kamikaze pilots in World War II believed that physical reality was not the ultimate reality; therefore, by sacrificing their lives for the cause of Japan, they would gain a better karma in the next life.[18] The worldview of Zen Buddhism, which dominated Japanese thinking during that time, dictated the actions, values, and choices of many of its soldiers who committed suicide rather than face the shame of surrender.

Or consider the actions of the executives at Enron and WorldCom in the early twenty-first century. Both of these organizations embraced the premise that growing quarterly earnings was a driving value; hence, if lies and deception were required to give the illusion of growing earnings, so be it. Of course in the end, the investment community let it be known that the values practiced by Enron and WorldCom were not acceptable.

Every person has a value system that is rooted in his or her worldview. When a person is hired, the worldview and values of that person are part of the package. It is therefore incumbent on managers to hire people whose worldview lines up with that of the organization. Southwest Airlines is one organization that understands this reality. The hiring policy is characterized as "hiring for attitude."[19] By this Southwest means that attitude, which is a reflection of character, is one of the most critical components to look for in the hiring process. Attitude reflects one's worldview, which is difficult to change; hence, Southwest doesn't try to change it. They hire people who are aligned with them in character and values.

King Solomon, who was given wisdom by God[20] and arguably the wisest human who has ever lived, tells us that the foundation for wisdom is *"the fear of the Lord."*[21] This is another way of saying "biblical worldview." When a person has God's perspective, that person will align his or her life with God's principles and values. If an employer is wise, he or she will seek to hire people that are aligned with God's principles and values because alignment with God brings blessing. Note the Lord's directive to Israel as they were preparing to enter the Promised Land:

> *Walk in all the way that the LORD your God has commanded*
> *you, so that you may live and prosper and prolong your days*
> *in the land that you will possess.*[22]

If this principle is true of the Israelites entering the Promised Land, is it not still true today?

Capability

Of King David, it was said: "And David shepherded them with integrity of heart; with skillful hands he led them."[23] The term "skillful hands" refers to David's capability. Capability is the combination of one's experience, training, aptitudes, and behavior pattern that facilitates doing tasks and/or relating to people. Being skillful at something means that one is very good—even world-class—at that something. If one believes in personal destiny by an intelligent Creator, it is logical to assume that one's capability should be congruent with one's destiny. That is, if God created David to be a king, then He gifted David to rule.

> IF ONE BELIEVES IN PERSONAL DESTINY BY AN INTELLIGENT CREATOR, IT IS LOGICAL TO ASSUME THAT ONE'S CAPABILITY SHOULD BE CONGRUENT WITH ONE'S DESTINY.

Every person has specific skills that facilitate his or her ability to accomplish tasks and/or relate to others. Since skills are the components most easily understood, many employers focus on the skills needed for a position. However, skills are just one of the C4 components and probably no more important than the others. Wise employers learn to value all of the C4 components in making hiring decisions. One example of skills is human aptitude.

In 1922, General Electric established a research program known as the Human Engineering Laboratory. Johnson O'Connor was the first director.[24] The purpose of this facility was to understand the human traits that facilitated excellence in doing different tasks. With time, the laboratory was moved into a separate nonprofit foundation and the research continues to this day.

From this research, a theory of human aptitudes developed. The following is a list of these aptitudes.[25]

Graphoria (clerical speed)	Rhythm memory
Ideaphoria (flow of ideas)	Memory for design
Foresight (seeing possibilities)	Silograms (word learning)
Inductive reasoning	Number memory
Analytical reasoning	Observation
Structural visualization	Finger dexterity
Number facility	Tweezer dexterity
Tonal memory	Subjective (loner)/
Pitch discrimination	objective (team player)

According to aptitude theory, for any particular task or job to be done well, there is an optimum combination of aptitudes. For example, tonal memory, rhythm memory, and pitch discrimination are the aptitudes for a musician. Finger dexterity, tweezer dexterity, and inductive reasoning are aptitudes that world-class surgeons possess. Analytical reasoning and foresight are aptitudes of business leaders.

Every human being has a unique blend of aptitudes. No one is strong in all the aptitudes. Each person possesses a combination of aptitudes that enables him or her to efficaciously carry out his or her assigned mission. Because of this reality, great organizations consist of teams of people with complementary skills.

In addition to aptitudes, every human has a behavior pattern commonly know as a personality profile. Unlike aptitude theory which is a fairly recent field of study, personality theory dates back two thousand years. Though there are many models, each model posits human behavior in terms of four key characteristics. The DISC model, promulgated by Inscape Publishing, is a typical model. DISC stands for dominance, inspirational, steadiness, and compliance. A person high in dominance is a no-nonsense, result-oriented individual. An inspirational person loves people and fun. Steady people value peace and predictability. Compliant people want to do things right.

According to personality theory, every human being possesses a blend of the four components. Individual behavior is primarily determined by the two most dominant components of a person's personality profile. A key factor in determining the capability of any person is to understand the individual's personality profile, since the personality profile determines the behavior pattern of the individual.

During the latter part of the 1990s, the J. C. Penney Company engaged in a major restructuring. One of the store managers came to see me. His personality profile was an S-C, which means that he was into doing the routine right. This is a great profile to maintain the status quo. However, the company, was seeking to effect change. The company delegated the restructuring to people with high D personalities, which is wise since change is the name of the game for high Ds. These individuals tend to get the job done; frequently, however, there is little sensitivity to people. Needless to say, the S-C manager, who is not a change agent, was having a difficult time with the tactics of the high D change agents. During lunch that day, I explained personality theory to the manager. Armed with an understanding of his personality, the manager was able to develop a plan to transition the restructuring, which enabled him to survive the chaos of change until peace and routine could be restored.

Aptitudes and personality are not the only components that define human capability. For example, there are different thinking processes sometimes referred to as *right brain, left brain,* and *whole brain.* Right brain refers to intuitive and creative thinking. Left brain refers to cognitive and analytic thinking. Whole brain thinking is the balance of the left and right brain.

Also, each of us has different education, training, experiences, and interests. There are also different learning styles, such as kinesthetic, auditory, visual, and contemplative. With regard to preferring people or tasks, there are three options. Introverts choose tasks over people. Extraverts prefer people over tasks. Ambiverts don't have a preference. Some people are team players and others are loners. There are physical differences in athletic ability and coordination. To a varying degree, each of us has an intangible quality commonly known as intuition or feel. In any decision there is a gut-check or emotional component that should be considered.

All of these various components combine to determine our capability. No two humans are the same. Though we are all here to rule the physical world, each of us has a different role to play. May we each find that place where our skill serves us well, and may we experience what was said of King David:

> And David shepherded them with integrity of heart; with skillful hands he led them.[26]

Commissioning

The dictionary definition of *commission* is an authorization or command to act in a prescribed manner or to perform prescribed acts. When one is commissioned to do something, one is given authorization to do certain acts by someone in authority over that person. For example, King David commissioned his son, Solomon, to build the temple.[27] When King Saul was seeking someone to play the harp for him, David was commissioned by his father to serve Saul[28] as his harpist. My wife was commissioned by her father to be a teacher. She tried numerous activities before deciding to focus on teaching. She had a modicum of success doing these various activities, but when she turned her focus to teaching, she enjoyed great success and found unmatched personal satisfaction.

For most of us, our commissioning comes from our fathers. It can also come from teachers, employers, pastors, and so forth. Anyone who has some level of authority over a person can speak a commissioning statement. A commissioning statement is simply an affirmation to do the work one is called to do. For my wife, it was a statement by her father that she should be a teacher.

Commissioning is the external validation that we all need in order to do what we think we are called to do. A person who has not been commissioned is not confident, even if that person has a sense of calling. When confidence is lacking, a person does not press through the inevitable obstacles to fulfill his or her calling.

When the apostles selected people to handle the food distribution to the early church in Jerusalem, these men were commissioned by the apostles to perform this task.[29] This example implies that workplace activities, such as food distribution, are important. People need to be commissioned to perform these tasks.

COMMISSIONING IS THE EXTERNAL VALIDATION THAT WE ALL NEED IN ORDER TO DO WHAT WE THINK WE ARE CALLED TO DO.

No one can self-commission. Commissioning requires someone in authority to call out one's life purpose. When people are not commissioned, doubt impairs them and blocks them from fulfilling their destiny. One of the greatest blessings any father can bestow on his children is to commission them. Commissioning our children requires us to study and seek to understand God's purpose and destiny for them, and to proactively and positively call that destiny out.

C4 in Practice

When I was in high school, I knew three brothers who were very close. Unlike most brothers of that time, they did everything together. They were great friends and supported each other. The middle brother and youngest brother were on the high school golf team with me. The youngest one was the most capable player on the team. He had a wonderful athletic swing, a smooth flowing rhythm that was the envy of the rest of us, but he had no heart for the game. The only reason that he played was to be with his brother. Though his capability allowed him to develop a wonderful golf swing, he was not called to play golf. His heart was to be a creative artist. Today, he owns an artistic furniture studio and is very content and successful.

The challenge for each of us is to find our C4 job—the place and work where the full expression of our calling, character, capability, and commissioning can be released. My thesis is that when one finds the place where one's C4 is allowed to be fully expressed, then one excels and finds great contentment. I say "place," because not only is *what* we do important, but *where* we do it is equally important. The selection of where we work is critical to minimize conflict and maximize productive work.

Frequently, I go into companies and ask CEOs and business owners a simple question. How many people in your organization are functioning at a high level? In other words, how many have a passion for what they are doing and are doing a really outstanding job? Almost always the answer is the same: very few. By this, they typically mean much less than 10 percent. It is a sad reality that few people are working in their C4 jobs.

The difficulty of finding one's C4 job should not be underestimated. For many, it is a lifelong pursuit, sometimes consciously and other times unconsciously. There seems to be something designed by the Creator in the fabric of humans that drives us. The challenge is to unlock the drive. In the days immediately after the space shuttle exploded in February 2003, I recall hearing a number of reports about the dedication of the astronauts to their profession and how they did not view being an astronaut as a job but as a calling. A comment was made that they worked out of passion—not for money. Looking over the spectrum of people that I have served through the years, there are few of whom it could be said that they worked out of passion, not for money.

> **THE CHALLENGE FOR EACH OF US IS TO FIND OUR C4 JOB.**

In my experience, my wife is one of the greatest examples of someone who is working in her C4 job. The evidence is abundant. She eagerly rises early in the morning to do her exercise and have her quiet time before leaving at 6:50 A.M. to go to school. At school, she continually enjoys favor with the students, faculty, administration, and parents; she is highly regarded. She works for internal satisfaction, not for money. Clearly, she feels called to teach. Her character is aligned with the values and principles of the private Christian school where she works. She has well-honed teaching skills. And as a young girl, her father commissioned her to teach. I can say unequivocally that she is in her C4 work.

Equally Yoked C4 Senior Leaders

For an organization to function at a high level of excellence, it must be led by senior leaders who are equally yoked based on their individual C4. This means that each member of senior leadership must have a heart to work together. Their worldviews are in alignment: they have the same view of reality, share the same values, and operate on the same principles. Each of the senior leaders brings a needed and complementary skill set so that the combination of skills is clearly superior to anyone's individual skills. And each member of the senior team is commissioned to do what he or she is doing; each functions out of a confident and tenacious sense of purpose.

The sad reality is that, in my experience, there are few organizations that have senior leaders who are equally yoked. As a result, most organizations suffer from ineffective leadership. For example, I know of an organization that has a very dysfunctional and ineffective team member who lacks C4 to be in senior leadership. The CEO knows this, but is so driven by mercy that he will not confront the reality and blocks the attempts of other senior leaders to properly deal with the matter. This creates conflict, distraction, and inefficiency among the senior leaders.

The ripple effect in the organization is evident. The organization is on a plateau and, arguably, it is going backward. It is no longer growing and is suffering financial difficulties. Despite the clear indicators that something is wrong, the CEO's dysfunction blocks the efforts of the other senior leaders to deal with the unequally yoked team member. In light of what is actually happening, perhaps even the CEO leader lacks C4 to run this organization. That is, his character is not sufficient to make the hard decisions that are in the best interest of the organization as a whole. The CEO's personal agenda is trumping the organization's agenda. Anytime a personal agenda trumps the good of the organization, the organization cannot function with singular purpose and excellence.

In another organization, the CEO inherited his job because he was the son of the founder. This CEO does not have the C4 to lead the organization. The founder probably knew that his son was not qualified, but lacked the courage to be honest with his own son. With a CEO lacking the C4 to perform his job, the organization, once highly respected and profitable, declined. It was rescued from the precipice of bankruptcy by means of a friendly acquisition.

In these real-life scenarios, each organization's ability to achieve excellence was thwarted by senior leaders who were unequally yoked. In each example, at least one senior leader either lacked C4 or lost his or her C4. Furthermore, the other senior leaders failed or were unable to deal with the situation.

One can represent the level of efficiency in a management team according to the following equation:

$$\text{EFFICIENCY} = \frac{\text{ENERGY AVAILABLE TO PERFORM WORK}}{\text{TOTAL ENERGY OF THE SYSTEM}}$$

$$\text{TOTAL ENERGY OF THE SYSTEM} = \text{ENERGY AVAILABLE TO PERFORM WORK} + \text{BALANCING ENERGY}$$

"Balancing energy" represents the energy spent on balancing the yoked system. Every yoked system uses part of the total energy to keep itself in balance. The key to efficiency is to minimize the energy required to maintain balance.

When a team of senior leaders ignores unequal yoking, the team naturally and often subconsciously seeks to compensate for the deficiency. The team starts covering for the dysfunctional leader or leaders. This compensation effort (balancing energy) takes useful energy away from productive work, leading to a significant reduction in efficiency. As a result, the organization is unable to deliver an excellent value proposition. Without excellence, no organization will prosper over the long term.

Levels of Leaders

Another model for the assessment of equal yoking is that proposed by Jim Collins. In his research to determine what makes organizations transition from good to great, Mr. Collins defines five levels of leaders.[30]

Level 1 – personal competence
Level 2 – contributing team player
Level 3 – competent manager
Level 4 – effective, though self-centered, leader
Level 5 – humble, selfless, tenacious leader

Level 4 and 5 leaders are the senior leaders of an organization. Based on working with a plethora of organizations over the past three decades, my observation is that most senior leaders are Level 4. Level 4 leaders are impaired in their long-term ability to produce excellence because of sin. Their sin is pride and narcissism. To confirm my observation note what Jack Trifts, dean of the University of Southern Maine School of Business, states about publicly held companies: "The myth of American corporate governance is that these companies are run by managers for shareholders, with nothing in mind but the good of those shareholders. That and a fairy godmother giving you money for your teeth are of the same ilk."[31]

One of my clients is a rapidly growing organization that made the mistake of building its management team too quickly. As a result, the overhead exceeded the company's cash flow capability. The company endured losses for a number of months, hoping that business would align with expectations, but it never did. Finally, the CEO requested ideas from the management team to bring alignment between revenue and expenses.

Every member of the management team, except one, volunteered to cut his or her compensation substantially. The one who didn't frustrated the CEO with his insistence that everyone else take a pay cut except him. Such an attitude is that of a Level 4 leader whose personal agenda trumps what's best for the organization. The CEO terminated this person, which illustrates what frequently happens to Level 4 leaders. Level 4 leaders are not viewed as critical resources by organizations that are truly seeking enduring excellence.

Why do Level 4 leaders fail? Sydney Finkelstein explores why smart executives fail and astutely articulates the reasons why. He notes that smart people who dramatically fail typically display the following manifestations of pride:[32]

- They see themselves and their companies as dominating their environments.

- They identify so completely with the company that there is no clear boundary between their personal interests and their corporation's interests.

- They think they have all the answers.

- They ruthlessly eliminate anyone who isn't 100 percent behind them.

- They are consummate company spokespersons, obsessed with the company image.

- They underestimate major obstacles.

- They stubbornly rely on what worked for them in the past.

Although Dr. Finkelstein doesn't connect his work to that of Jim Collins, the mistakes listed above would be mistakes made by Level 4 leaders. On the other hand, Level 5 leaders are characterized by the qualities of humbleness and tenacity. This does not mean that Level 5 leaders are without sin; rather they are mature enough to defer their personal agendas for the good of the organization.

In a *Star Trek* movie, there is a scene where Spock, the consummate logician, sacrifices his life to save the spaceship. After saving the ship and in the process of dying, he has a final conversation with Captain Kirk. Spock states that his actions were logical because the "good of the many outweighs the good of the one." This perspective epitomizes Level 5 thinking.

During Jack Welch's tenure as CEO of GE, he adopted a principle that he called "boundaryless."[33] By this he meant that everyone should be selfless in looking for great ideas. If one is infected by "the not thought of here" syndrome, one limits one's creativity to one's self. Mr. Welch recognized that God created a wide variety of human aptitudes. By embracing the wealth found in the diverse human aptitudes, Welch sought to find the best ideas for every problem that GE faced. This perspective is Level 5 thinking. Personal pride is subordinated to the goal of finding the best solution for every problem, regardless of the source of the solution.

The concept of Level 5 leaders is noble. Level 5 leaders are rare, however, because we humans are naturally narcissistic. Fred Smith, CEO of FedEx, notes the following about people:

> When people walk in the door, they want to know: What do you expect out of me? What's in this deal for me? What do I have to do to get ahead? Where do I go in this organization to get justice if I'm not treated appropriately? They want to know how they're doing. They want some feedback. And they want to know that what they are doing is important. If you take the basic principles of leadership and answer those questions over and over again, you can be successful dealing with people. The thing that I think is missing most in business is people who really understand how to deal with rank-and-file employees.[34]

Mr. Smith adroitly recognizes that people suffer from a self-centered perspective, which sounds a lot like the apostle Paul who argued that "all have sinned and fall short of the glory of God."[35] If Mr. Smith is going to successfully deal with his workers, he must start where they are and lead them to where he wants them to go. In other words, he must meet their needs before they begin to meet the needs of FedEx and its customers. Level 5 thinking can be embedded in organizations where Level 5 leaders make it a strategic objective to do so. When Level 5 leadership functions this way, the whole organization experiences equal yoking that leads to organizational excellence and prosperity.

In my experience, Level 5 leaders seem to be rare. Abraham Lincoln, president of the United States, understood the importance of a unified nation and was willing to sacrifice to maintain a union. John Wanamaker, the father of the modern department store, pioneered many of the modern methods for doing business. R. G. LeTourneau started in the dirt-moving business and built an empire based on efficiency, productivity, and excellence. Sam Walton brought value to the consumer as no one else had. All of these men were willing to sacrifice personally to achieve organizational excellence. Such is the essence of Level 5 leadership.

Coupled with personal sacrifice, Level 5 leaders are eager learners. They are continually searching for truth and to bring their organizations into alignment with truth. King Josiah is a great illustration of a Level 5 leader. At age eight, he became king. At age sixteen, he began to seek God. At age twenty, he rid his domain of idols. At age twenty-six, he began rebuilding the temple, discovered the law, and brought his domain into alignment with God's revelation.[36] Josiah demonstrated how being faithful in a little leads to more revelation. He also demonstrated the power of exercising dominion in his sphere of authority.

The ultimate Level 5 leader obeys the two great commandments given in the Bible: to love God and to love your neighbor as yourself.[37] These are the highest of all commandments; all other principles and values flow out of these two commandments. Furthermore, Level 5 leaders display the tenacious humility that Jim Collins refers to by obeying the commandment of Jesus to die to self.[38] Personal agendas must be subordinated to the good of the organization.

An equally yoked team of Level 5 leaders is powerful. Imagine a team of selfless learners operating in the principle of love who are always looking for the best ideas to solve every problem. What a powerful leadership team! There would be minimal conflict, which would enable most of the energy of the team to be used to produce results. Such teams would operate at a high level of efficiency, producing excellent products and services that transform societies and individuals.

Conclusion

What organization will not, at least publicly, state that it wants to be excellent? I have never known an organization to admit that it wants to be mediocre. The objective of every management team that I have had the privilege of knowing is to be the best. So how does an organization become the best? It becomes the best by building according to God's philosophy, values, and principles.

A key biblical principle that facilitates excellence in organizational management is unified, equally yoked senior leadership. This means that those yoked together have, as a foundation, a compatible biblical worldview and unity of purpose. Building on this, those yoked together need complementary gifts plus equal capability, maturity, and motivation. A breakdown in any of these components will compromise the management team's ability to achieve excellence.

There is a maxim that an organization with a poor product but great management will beat an organization with a great product and poor management. This is true because excellent organizations must have great senior management teams. Great management teams are those that are equally yoked based on C4—calling, character, capability, and commissioning. These teams have a diverse blend of Level 5 leaders—humble but tenacious men and women of integrity. Level 5 leaders always put the organization's interests ahead of their personal agendas. Organizations led by teams like this cannot help but possess excellence.

Henry Parsons Crowell, founder of the Quaker Oats Company, believed strongly in the importance of equal yoking based on a biblical worldview. Joe Musser, Crowell's biographer, wrote:

He knew the value and validity of his faith and beliefs and how these had been the basis for his entire life of business and Christian enterprises. Now, he understood, it was not enough that believers put godly men and women into positions of leadership. These godly people must also surround themselves with others who share their beliefs. If someone is hired who is not of faith, he has the opportunity to bring down all the work which others have erected before him.[39]

The degree to which any organization aligns itself with a biblical worldview is directly proportional to the long-term success that the organization will enjoy. The more completely an organization is yoked together with the Creator, the more revelation is imparted to the organization. Truly excellent organizations, either wittingly or unwittingly, are yoked at some level with the Creator. Only from this place does lasting, world-class organizational excellence emanate.

Points to Ponder

1. Relative to your current job, are you called (do you have passion) to do the work? Do you have strong enough biblical character to do it well? Do you have the required capability? Have you been commissioned and released to do it? In other words, do you have C4?

2. Are you equally yoked at work? If not, in what ways are you unequally yoked?

3. Give an example of an unequally yoked organization. What were, or are, the symptoms of unequal yoking in the organization? What should be done to correct the problem?

Notes

1. Psalms 133.
2. Amos 3:3.
3. Mark 3:25.
4. 2 Corinthians 6:14–16.
5. 2 Corinthians 6:1–13.
6. Psalms 106:28.
7. Matthew 11:25–30.
8. Genesis 11:1–9.
9. Deuteronomy 22:10.
10. Michael E. Gerber, *The E-Myth Revisited* (NY: HarperBusiness, 2001), 2.

11. Jim Collins, *Good to Great* (NY: HarperBusiness, 2001), 74.

12. Ibid., 42, 50.

13. Isaiah 46:10.

14. Luke 2:49 (KJV).

15. Nehemiah 2:12.

16. Exodus 36:2 (KJV).

17. C. William Pollard, *The Soul of the Firm* (NY: HarperBusiness, 1996), 25.

18. Marvin Olasky, "Coverage of Buddhism," *World Magazine*, 8 March 2003.

19. Freiberg, *Nuts*, 66–69.

20. 2 Chronicles 1:12.

21. Proverbs 1:7.

22. Deuteronomy 5:33.

23. Psalms 78:22.

24. Dean Trembly, *Learning to Use Your Aptitudes* (The Johnson O'Connor Research Foundation, 1995), 2.

25. Ibid., 2.

26. Psalms 78:72.

27. 1 Chronicles 28.

28. 1 Samuel 16:20.

29. Acts 6:6.

30. Collins, *Good to Great*, chapter 2.

31. *Portland Press Herald*, 8 July 2003.

32. Sydney Finkelstein, *Why Smart Executives Fail* (NY: Penguin Group, 2003), 213–237.

33. Jack Welch, *Jack:Straight from the Gut* (NY: Warner Business Books, 2001), chapter 13.

34. Charles Fishman, "Face Time with Fred Smith," *Fast Company*, Issue 47, June 2001, p.64.

35. Romans 3:23.

36. 2 Chronicles 34.

37. Matthew 22:36–40.

38. Matthew 16:24.

39. Joe Musser, *The Cereal Tycoon* (Chicago: Moody Press, 1997), 145.

Beyond Babel Model

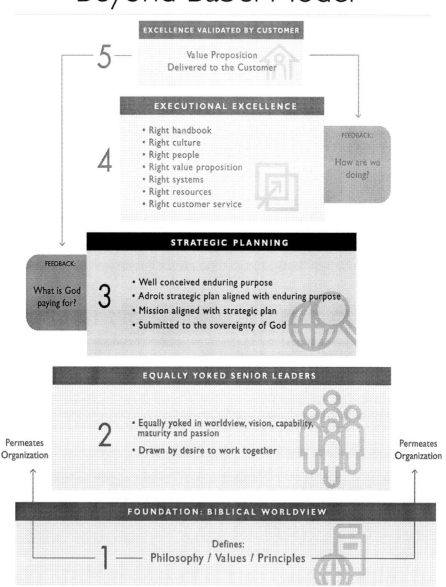

EXCELLENCE VALIDATED BY CUSTOMER

5 — Value Proposition
Delivered to the Customer

EXECUTIONAL EXCELLENCE

4
- Right handbook
- Right culture
- Right people
- Right value proposition
- Right systems
- Right resources
- Right customer service

FEEDBACK:

How are we doing?

STRATEGIC PLANNING

FEEDBACK:

What is God paying for?

3
- Well conceived enduring purpose
- Adroit strategic plan aligned with enduring purpose
- Mission aligned with strategic plan
- Submitted to the sovereignty of God

EQUALLY YOKED SENIOR LEADERS

Permeates Organization

2
- Equally yoked in worldview, vision, capability, maturity and passion
- Drawn by desire to work together

Permeates Organization

FOUNDATION: BIBLICAL WORLDVIEW

1 — Defines:
Philosophy / Values / Principles

Strategic Planning

Be an Ace

Everyone knows what it means to ace an exam, ace a project, or ace an interview. It means that you did really well. In part, Webster's online dictionary defines *ace:* "a point scored especially on a service (as in tennis or handball) that an opponent fails to touch; a golf score of one stroke on a hole; a combat pilot who has brought down at least five enemy airplanes; and one that excels at something."

An ace is the most valuable card in a deck of cards. An ace is one who is regarded as a pro at whatever he or she does. Being an ace connotes mastery of something and performance at a high level.

The idea of being an ace appeals to most of us because there is something in us that wants to perform at a high level. Most of us have enjoyed an experience being an ace in some context. Sometimes we may view our performance as luck, like making a hole in one in golf. But to ace anything involves some measure of skill and preparation.

Queen Esther: Ace

Being an ace at anything is the process of turning vision into reality. No one can really excel at anything without a vision for what he or she wants to achieve. Solomon tells us that "Where there is no vision, the people perish."[1]

> **NO ONE CAN REALLY EXCEL AT ANYTHING WITHOUT A VISION FOR WHAT HE OR SHE WANTS TO ACHIEVE.**

In other words, when we don't have a revelation of why we are here and what we are here to do, there is no life in us. The story of Queen Esther illustrates this point.

Having been granted the royal position of queen after Vashti defied the will of the king, Esther found her people, the Jews, under a judgment of death at the wicked hands of Haman. Knowing that the king endorsed Haman's edict and that the king's endorsement could not be rescinded, she was at a crossroads. Her cousin Mordecai provided the vision she needed. He noted that she, of all the Jews, was in a position to influence the king. The book of Esther records Mordecai's challenge to Esther to think beyond herself and risk her life to save her people:

> *"Do not think that because you are in the king's house you alone of all the Jews will escape. For if you remain silent at this time, relief and deliverance for the Jews will arise from another place, but you and your father's family will perish. And who knows but that you have come to royal position for such a time as this?"*[2]

Esther embraced the challenge and immediately began clarifying the vision. To clarify the vision, she needed to understand how to bring deliverance to the Jews. Specifically, she had to persuade the king to issue another edict that would allow the Jews to defend themselves. Having clarified the vision, she needed a plan that embraced the brutal reality of the pending demise of the Jews, but facilitated turning the vision of saving the Jews into reality. A key step in the plan was to gain an audience with the king that could have been her demise had the king not granted that she live. In the end, Esther was the vessel of deliverance. She turned vision into reality by acquiring vision, clarifying vision, and executing the vision. In other words, she was an ace.

An ace is someone who:
A – acquires a vision
C – clarifies the vision
E – executes the vision

John Wanamaker: Ace

Another ace was John Wanamaker. He was born in Philadelphia in 1838. Early in life, John had a vision for the retail business, and throughout his life he clarified and executed this vision. At the age of twelve he had a defining moment while buying his mother a Christmas gift at a jewelry store. After making a selection and while the storekeeper was wrapping the gift, John saw an item that he thought his mother would like better. The storekeeper rebuffed his effort to exchange the gift. This experience profoundly affected John. He resolved that when he owned his own store, he would treat people kindly and fairly. At sixteen he was hired to clean brass knobs at an upscale men's clothing store. Soon he moved into sales and then became manager.

At twenty-three, he opened his own store with his brother-in-law in 1861. His brother-in-law died, and in 1872 John became the sole owner of the largest retail store in the country. In 1876 he combined a number of specialty stores into one facility, creating the world's first department store. But this wasn't his only "first."

He pioneered price tags, single pricing, merchandise guarantees, written receipts, and returns and exchanges. He was the first retailer to use electric lights and to air condition his store. In addition, he provided weather forecasts, telegraph service, employee benefits (vacation, education assistance, health care, pension, and life insurance), and music in the store. Other pioneering practices were newspaper ads and white sales. In all of this, he never forgot his driving vision of treating customers fairly and kindly.

The starting point for an ace is vision. Vision is rooted in the heart. John's experience of buying a gift for his mother, though negative, put a vision and resolve in his heart. He determined that he was going to have a store and treat people kindly and fairly. Not everyone has a vision. Many young people go to college with very little vision for their lives. I have seen people in their forties and fifties with very little sense of destiny and purpose. These people are typically frustrated with life and tend to drift aimlessly.

VISION IS ATTAINED BY DILIGENTLY SEEKING OUT WHY WE WERE CREATED.

Some people enter into a phase commonly known as midlife crisis, characterized by regression to dreams of younger days. People in this phase don't display clarity of vision. A common vision in America today is retirement: work hard for forty or fifty years and retire. Better yet, win the lottery and thumb your nose at your job as you go to pick up your check. I'm being facetious. The point is that many of us do not have a significant vision for our lives. Vision is attained by diligently seeking out why we were created. Within each of us there is a longing to know who we are, why we are here, and what we are designed to do. It is such a fundamental component of the human condition that acquiring vision appears to be a prerequisite for finding peace and contentment.

But having vision is not enough. The vision must be sharpened and focused. John Wanamaker spent his life clarifying his vision. He began with a vision to be in the retail business and to treat people kindly and fairly. Then there was the vision to own a store that developed into the vision of a department store. All of these steps were part of the process of clarifying vision. For all of us, clarifying our vision is a heuristic (trial and error) process. The challenge is to correctly interpret our experiences, discover our strengths and weaknesses, and find where we have favor. John undoubtedly experienced failures along the way, but he chose to learn from those mistakes. Like all of us, John naturally gravitated to what he did well and sought to avoid what he didn't do well. This illustrates a fundamental principle about how God creates people. God gives gifts to each person congruent with His purpose for that person. Each person must assume responsibility to search out his or her calling and destiny, which is the process of clarifying vision.

This clarification process is an ongoing lifelong activity. It requires commitment, focus, and tenacity. In addition, it requires help and input from others. Everyone needs input and perspective from others. The president of the United States does not make major decisions without input from advisors. In the context of finding one's life purpose, advisors are people who offer different perspectives of a person's gifts and talents. It is these different perspectives that help a person find his or her life purpose.

Clarifying one's life purpose is a heuristic process. Trial and error is a marvelous opportunity for each person to better understand his or her gifts and talents. This means that failures can be an important guide for people and, in some cases, failures are as important as a person's successes.

Circumstances also play an important role. Many times events happen outside one's control, but these events shape and direct one's life. If the God of the Bible is the sovereign God of Creation, one must believe that God is revealing purpose and destiny for individuals through circumstances. Queen Esther's opportunity to save the Jewish people was set up by the circumstances of the day.

A corollary of circumstances is favor. Favor is experienced when opportunities come, many times unexpectedly and without explanation. The challenge is to recognize and embrace favor. Also, favor flows as a person submits to God's philosophy, values, and principles. Note what the Lord says to the nation of Israel:

> *Now if you obey me fully and keep my covenant, then out of all nations you will be my treasured possession. Although the whole earth is mine.*[3]

What incredible favor to be the Lord's treasured possession.

Once a person's vision is clarified, it's time to execute. Adroit execution starts with an honest assessment of the current condition and a clear vision as to where to go. Then a plan is mapped out to transition from where a person is to where the person wants to go. John Wanamaker was a master executer. He didn't act until he had clear vision, but when he had that vision, he moved decisively and without fear.

Moving without fear is challenging for all of us. We fear failure, loss, rejection, pain, and so on. Fear can paralyze any attempts to execute vision in our lives. An ace never lets fear get in the way. An ace clearly sees the vision, skillfully develops a plan of action, and executes it fearlessly—regardless of the pain in the process. Tom Landry, legendary former coach of the Dallas Cowboys, once stated that setting a goal is not the main thing. The main thing is deciding how you will go about achieving the goal, and then not letting the pain of the process required to achieve the goal, stop you.

Benjamin Martin: Ace

In the movie *The Patriot,* Mel Gibson played Benjamin Martin, a South Carolina pacifist who lost his wife, two sons, and a daughter-in-law. His wife was lost before the War of Independence, and the British killed the others during the war. Having witnessed the death of one of his young sons by the cruel hand of British Colonel Tavington, Ben Martin quickly turned from a pacifist into a fighting patriot. He acquired a vision. Throughout the movie, Ben clarified and executed, moving ever closer to the vision of independence.

> **AN ACE CLEARLY SEES THE VISION, SKILLFULLY DEVELOPS A PLAN OF ACTION, AND EXECUTES IT FEARLESSLY.**

In the final battle of the movie, Ben and his archenemy Colonel Tavington squared off for an individual contest in the midst of battle. Ben came into the engagement battle weary from fighting and heavyhearted from the loss of his two sons to the tyrannical British colonel. Tavington used cruel and inhuman tactics, targeting civilians for death as the penalty for helping the rebels. Now in mortal combat as he sought to fulfill his vision of killing the colonel, Ben found himself in a precarious position. The colonel struck several blows, causing Ben to fall to his knees. Exhausted and drained, Ben waited for the deathblow when he suddenly saw the colonial battle flag.

The visual image stirred his heart as he remembered that the battle was not about his exhaustion, but about securing freedom for his remaining family and friends from the tyranny of the British crown. Refocused, he mustered strength to rejoin the battle and gained victory over the despotic British colonel.

Ben Martin was an ace. He acquired vision. The vision was clarified by the death of two sons and a daughter-in-law. He knew that his family could not survive under the cruel tyranny of the British, and so he fought for independence. His planning and implementation were skillful, but he encountered many obstacles. Recruiting and training local militia was arduous. The British were better equipped and trained. They also surprised Ben with some of their tactics. The death of Ben's oldest son proved to be nearly too much. But when he found the colonial battle flag among his son's belongings, this symbol of freedom from tyranny stirred his heart and refocused his resolve. The weariness and discouragement of life no longer gripped his heart. Instead the vision of freedom and liberty for his family was again in focus.

All of us need symbols to refocus us when the obstacles of life discourage and distract us. Symbols can be visual, auditory, and/or aromatic. If you are a Christian, the cross and the Lord's Supper are powerful symbols of the Christian faith. Also, great hymns like "Amazing Grace" stir our hearts. Citizens of the United States are moved by the Pledge of Allegiance, the flag, and the national anthem. Organizations frequently have flags, tag lines, logos, company songs, and company smells (for example, Mrs. Field's cookies) to stir vision and focus.

When GE's customers complained about the tube quality of the CT scan machines, GE, as part of the strategy for improved quality, posted signs all throughout the manufacturing facility with the slogan "Tubes—The Heart of the System."[4] A symbol can be anything that reminds us of our vision. It can be our mission statement on the wall in our office, a picture of a new product, a company song, a scent, or a piece of art—anything that enables one to overcome one's frailties and press through the battle to victory.

> **"VISION IS THE ABILITY TO SEE IT, THE FAITH TO BELIEVE IT, THE COURAGE TO DO IT, AND THE HOPE TO ENDURE UNTIL IT HAPPENS."**
> **– JAMES RYLE**

When properly seen, a person's specific vision is congruent with his specific calling. The symbols that stir and refocus each of us will be different since each of us has a unique life purpose. When hope was lost, Benjamin Martin was re-energized by the sight of the battle flag.

My wife, who teaches children to read, is moved to tears at the sight of sculptures of children reading. I am moved when I see people change and grow.

James Ryle wrote, "There is talk these days of vision. But vision is much more than a good idea that stirs the soul to temporary endeavors. Vision is the ability to see it, the faith to believe it, the courage to do it, and the hope to endure until it happens. Take any of these components away and vision fails. Each is vital and indispensable."[5]

The Bible gives us a wonderful vision:

> *Let us fix our eyes on Jesus, the author and perfecter of our faith, who for the joy set before him endured the cross, scorning its shame, and sat down at the right hand of the throne of God. Consider him who endured such opposition from sinful men, so that you will not grow weary and lose heart.*[6]

Living out the reality of this vision should be the heart of every Christian. It was the heart of John Wanamaker. In addition to turning vision into reality in his retail business, he acquired great vision in working for the cause of Christ in business and every other area of life. He assisted the YMCA, helped to start six churches, sponsored evangelistic crusades, and served for years as Sunday school superintendent in his church.

John Wanamaker was such an ace in all of life that on his death in 1922, the flags in Philadelphia were lowered, schools were closed, the newspaper called him the city's most eminent citizen, and his pallbearers included the governor of Pennsylvania, mayors of New York and Philadelphia, the chief justice of the Supreme Court, and Thomas Edison.

Strategic Planning Is About Being an Ace

Both individuals and organizations can be aces. In fact, being an ace as an organization requires an organization full of individual aces. No organization can achieve world-class status without focus and excellence. Focus and excellence happen when nothing impairs the organization's ability to execute. Some of the greatest organizational impairments are people who do not know their life purpose. Such people are confused and inefficient. A team of confused, inefficient people cannot deliver products and services with excellence.

Confused and inefficient people tend to be depressed, and distract others. More than 16 percent of workers in the United States suffer from clinical depression. These people typically don't stay at home. Instead, they go to work and become impediments to organizational efficiency, as other workers are distracted by seeking to help them. Researchers estimate that depressed workers cost corporate America $44 billion a year in lost time,[7] which is four times the cost of lost time because of employee illness.

Furthermore, this estimate does not consider the inefficiencies imposed on the workers seeking to help the depressed workers. Who pays for this? Ultimately the consumer of the products and services of corporate America pays since this cost is simply part of the expense structure. Clearly, if an organization is truly committed to excellence, it must be an ace and have individual aces in place at every level.

The methodology for becoming an ace is the same for both individuals and organizations. The key steps to becoming an ace are embodied in the strategic planning process.

Biblical Basis for Strategic Planning

The Bible provides ample guidance on planning. Note, for example, the following characteristics of planning:

Planning provides order. Every organization needs order and focus to facilitate its activities. Without order and focus, an organization wanders aimlessly and purposelessly.

Where there is no revelation, the people cast off restraint.[8]

Planning is our responsibility. Granted, God is sovereign over the affairs of men.[9] Nevertheless, He has chosen to give man the responsibility of planning.

To man belong the plans of the heart.[10]
In his heart a man plans his course.[11]
Many are the plans in a man's heart.[12]

Man must never lose sight of the sovereignty of God. The sovereignty of God is the mysterious attribute of God that is irreconcilable to human responsibility. Nevertheless, the Bible testifies abundantly to the reality of divine sovereignty. We humans must be willing to let God be God and not try to impose on Him the requirement that we understand all of His attributes. It must be okay with us that God is not fully comprehensible. Therefore, planning is always submitted to the Lord and to the mystery of His sovereign will; nevertheless, we are responsible to plan.

. . . from the LORD comes the reply of the tongue.[13]

. . . the Lord determines his steps.[14]

It is the LORD's purpose that prevails.[15]

The lot is cast into the lap, but its every decision is from the LORD.[16]

There is no wisdom, no insight, no plan that can succeed against the LORD.
The horse is made ready for the day of battle, but victory rests with the LORD.[17]

No one has all the wisdom. Every human being has strengths and weaknesses. Therefore, for any organization or individual to develop an adroit plan, it must task a diverse blend of skilled people who can look at all the issues relevant to the planning process with wisdom and discernment. From this collective wisdom, an adept plan can emerge. Note some testimony from the Bible:

Plans fail for lack of counsel, but with many advisers they succeed.[18]

Make plans by seeking advice.[19]

God creates each person with limitations. No one has all the gifts and perspectives. This makes us dependent upon each other to find the wisdom to make the best decisions both as individuals and organizations. According to King Solomon, those who try to function alone are fools:

He who trusts in himself is a fool, but he who walks in wisdom is kept safe.[20]

Planning provides a foundation for success—despite the fact that no plan is guaranteed to succeed. Trying to steer a parked car is useless; the car must be moving for the steering to be effective. Planning gets an organization moving toward its vision and enables the organization's leadership to make the necessary course corrections to facilitate success. The Bible provides hope for a successful result from proper planning and, by implication, execution.

The plans of the diligent lead to profit.[21]

Elements of Strategic Planning

Strategic planning is the process whereby the senior leaders of an organization envision the future of the organization and map out the steps to realize that future. At a minimum, an organization should have a strategic planning meeting once each year.

There are five key elements of strategic planning—vision, assessment, goals, execution, and accountability. Either wittingly or unwittingly, every ace practices these five elements.

1. Vision

Being an ace starts with vision. No organization can achieve excellence without vision. Vision is the articulation of dreams and hopes by the senior leaders of the organization. King Solomon said, *"Where there is no vision, the people perish."*[22] Vision gives a target to the organization that provides direction and focus.

In 1961, President Kennedy committed the National Aeronautics and Space Administration (NASA) to the vision of landing a man on the moon by the end of the decade. This vision provided NASA with direction and focus. Despite the incredulity of many and despite experiencing a major loss when Apollo 1 suffered an electrical fire that killed three astronauts in 1967, NASA rose to the challenge and achieved the goal.

Though the accident set the program back, the commitment to the vision was so strong that NASA quickly recovered. Interestingly, once NASA achieved its vision of landing a man on the moon in 1969, NASA's funding was gradually cut, which prompted layoffs and a decline in the space program.

Though the vision of President Kennedy was clear and compelling, it was shortsighted. Effective, enduring vision must be long term if an organization is going to exist beyond a person, goal, or project.

2. Assessment

Understanding the current condition of an organization is essential. The assessment is the starting point for change. Therefore, the management team of an organization must know and face the truth about the current state of the organization.

At the beginning of the twentieth century, the dominant means of transportation in the United States was the railroad. Soon the automobile, truck, and airplane became viable options for transporting people and products. The railroads were ideally positioned to embrace these new technologies. Instead, the management teams of all the railroads made a fatal mistake in assessing the current state of their business. First, they did not understand the business they were in and second, they did not understand the season of their business.

The reality was that they were not in the railroad business but the transportation business. However, believing that they were in the railroad business, they rejected the new transportation options. The truth was that the railroad was the best transportation option at the beginning of the twentieth century. As the twentieth century unfolded, however, railroad technology could not compete with the emerging technologies. The railroad companies failed to realize that they were in the winter of the dominance of the railroad as the best transportation technology. With the introduction of superior transportation options, it was just a matter of time before the new options would capture market share.

One hundred years ago, the major stock market companies were industrials, with railroads as a major force. Today, railroads are far less significant in the economy as the transportation industry is dominated largely by aviation driven companies such as Federal Express, Southwest Airlines, and United Parcel Service. Had senior management of the various railroad companies correctly assessed the state of their businesses in the early 1900s, they may well have been the dominant players in transportation today. Any organization that fails to understand the truth about its state of affairs and its position will experience a reality check.

3. Goals

Once an organization knows its vision and its current condition, it is ready to establish goals. The purpose of goals is to effect transformation. If an organization knows where it wants to go at some point in the future and where it is today, it must begin to systematically and progressively change. Goals are the tools to help organizations change. Goals have three characteristics.

- First, goals must be measurable. Measurability enables an organization to know if and when it has achieved the goal.

- Second, a goal must have a deadline. Deadlines provide accountability at specific points in time so that an organization knows when it has achieved a goal.

- And third, goals must be assigned to a person. Someone must take responsibility for and ownership of each goal. The owner of a goal is the person accountable to the other members of the organization for accomplishing the goal.

Goals that do not possess these three characteristics are simply wishes, and wishes don't frequently come true. Goals are specific action steps that an organization chooses to take to bring about the transformation required to make the vision of the organization a reality. In 1961, President Kennedy's vision of landing a man on the moon by the end of the decade and returning him safely had to be broken down into a series of measurable goals. Each goal possessed these three characteristics.

4. Execution

The weak link in strategic planning is execution. The work of vision casting, assessment, and goal setting is largely an intellectual exercise that is frequently done in the context of an annual strategic planning meeting. These meetings are energizing venues that facilitate organizational focus and bonding among the participants. However, once the meeting is over, the participants go back to the daily grind of life, where the tyranny of the urgent typically dictates the daily actions and priorities. When this happens, there is a big temptation to forget about the strategic goals.

As a result, many organizations fail to execute their goals. Failure to execute goals means that the organization does not realize its vision. Such organizations tend to be reactive rather than proactive. Reactive organizations always lag behind proactive organizations. Proactive organizations lead, reactive organizations follow. Proactive organizations are committed to the execution of their strategic plan, knowing that failure to do so could have serious consequences on the long-term prospects of the organization.

5. Accountability

Every organization needs accountability to achieve its goals. Accountability facilitates execution. Adroit organizations wittingly submit to accountability. The following are some practical accountability tips for executing an organization's strategic goals:

- Immediately after the annual planning meeting, each goal owner should schedule tactical planning meetings to develop a plan to execute each goal.

- Each goal owner should provide regular reports to the team regarding progress on each goal. E-mail is a great vehicle to accomplish this.

- Trying to work on goals in the midst of daily activities is very difficult; therefore, each goal owner should set aside dedicated time weekly or monthly to work on the goals.

- Schedule periodic meetings for the sole purpose of reviewing the strategic plan and providing updates on goals.

The senior leader should take responsibility for monitoring the accountability process. Without accountability, the probability that an organization will reach its goals drops significantly. In my experience, facilitating strategic planning for a wide variety of organizations, I have yet to see an efficacious strategic plan without a serious commitment to accountability.

Mission Statement

The strategic plan of most organizations is, generally, a lengthy document; it is helpful to be able to capture the heart of the plan in a simple easy-to-remember statement commonly known as a mission statement. Every employee should know the mission statement. It should provide a guiding light to keep everyone in the organization on target. For mission statements to be efficacious, organizations must demonstrate, by word and deed, the importance of the mission statement. Mission statements should be posted in facilities and written on communications of all types. The workers should be trained and retrained to understand the mission statement and its importance. Management at all levels must make it clear that they are using the mission statement to help stay on course. The key to successfully using a mission statement is to demonstrate by actions that it is important.

I suggest that a mission statement answer the following five questions:

1. Who is the organization?

This is a statement of the identity of the organization. Every organization functions based on its identity. In 2003, the United States invaded Iraq. The United States Army was tasked with occupying the country until a democratic self-government could be established, which meant that the army served as a police force immediately after the war was concluded. Early in the occupation, it was widely reported that the army was not prepared to do police work. The reason was that the army's identity did not encompass police work. The army is a military unit trained to conduct war operations, not a police unit. The United States Army functions out of its identity as a military unit that conducts military activities. It is not a peacekeeping organization and is not highly effective functioning in that role.

2. Whom does the organization serve?

This is a statement of the organization's target audience. No organization can be all things to all people. Excellent organizations are very focused on whom they serve. A private Christian school usually has a policy of selective admissions. The school recognizes that parents are responsible for the education of their children; the school is simply a tool to help parents educate their children. "Christian" implies that the school functions from a biblical worldview. Since the school wants to operate with excellence, it must be equally yoked with parents; the parents must agree with the worldview of the school. Requiring worldview alignment with the parents is a tool for the school to determine whom they are to serve. If the school accepts students from parents that don't accept a biblical worldview, the school and parents risk serious conflict because of different philosophies, principles, and values.

3. What does the organization do?

To achieve a high level of excellence requires a clear understanding of what products and/or services an organization should provide.

One of my clients is in the paving business. When I first met the owner of the company, his business was failing. The company had a negative net worth of $1 million. My first assignment was to develop a turnaround plan without putting the company into bankruptcy. As I analyzed the situation, it became abundantly clear that the company was trying to offer too many different products. Each of the different products required slightly different ways of doing business.

Paving streets was very different from repairing potholes in parking lots. Concrete work is very different from asphalt work. Public work is very different from private work. Large jobs are different from small jobs. The essence of the turnaround plan was to define a clear focus for the company— to define what the company was supposed to be doing. It clearly could not be all things to all customers.

I developed the plan and presented it to the owner. He took a hard swallow and agreed to give it a try. Six years later, the company's net worth was a positive $1 million. There was no bankruptcy filing. Vendors were paid. And the company was clearly focused on the products it was supposed to offer. As a result of this experience, the owner works hard to stay focused. As long as the company stays in its niche, it prospers.

At one time Wal-Mart offered the company a large maintenance contract. This was a great temptation. But as management compared the scope of the contract against what the company was really good at doing, it was clear that the Wal-Mart contract was not a good fit. It's hard to walk away from an opportunity like that, but there is no doubt that it was the right decision. The company continues to flourish today because it understands the "what" of its business.

4. How does the organization accomplish its mission?

Every organization has a methodology by which it delivers its products and/or services. Southwest Airlines is the perennial low cost producer in the airline industry. Efforts by other airlines to offer more expensive upscale service invariably fail. The majority of the flying public is not willing to pay for upscale services such as gourmet meals or first-class seating. Since inception, Southwest understood this reality and has never offered upscale services. Its methodology has always been, and continues to be, to function as the provider of low-cost transportation services. The evidence of the wisdom of this methodology is that Southwest is the only airline that consistently makes a profit.

5. Why does the organization do what it does?

No organization exists without a reason or motivation for existing. There are many potential reasons. Some exist to make money. Others exist to make a name or to exert power and influence. Still others exist because of ego and hubris. And some exist because the founders felt called to build the organization or make a contribution to society. For some there is a confluence of reasons. But whatever the reason or reasons, every organization needs to be honest enough with itself to identify the driving motivation of the organization.

I have the privilege of supporting a charity by the name of Mercy Med+Flight (MMF). As of this writing, it is the only charitable air ambulance service in the United States. MMF provides free air ambulance transportation to those in desperate need that have no means to pay for the service. Several have tried to start a comparable service, but none has succeeded. The reason MMF has succeeded is the motivation of the founding stakeholders, specifically, the president.

Though MMF is a nonprofit organization, the president displays the dedication and commitment of an entrepreneur. He works tirelessly to overcome obstacles. Why does he do this for an organization that he doesn't own? The answer is his motivation. He has a heart for the mission of MMF. Seeing hurting, desperate people find help though MMF moves him to go the extra mile to insure the success of MMF in carrying out its humanitarian mission.

Strategic Boundaries

Every excellent organization must have a strategic plan and a mission statement to provide focus and direction. The mission statement provides the boundaries to guide daily decisions. Every day most of us have many ideas that sound really grand. Some of these ideas are great opportunities, while others are distractions. The challenge is to be able to distinguish between the two.

THE MISSION STATEMENT PROVIDES THE BOUNDARIES TO GUIDE DAILY DECISIONS.

One of my clients is in the pet service business. Providing nonmedical services to pet owners is a small, highly fragmented industry. As one might expect, there are few software applications available to support businesses of this type. Therefore, my client commissioned a software company to write custom software for the business. The software was excellent. In fact, it was so good that my client decided to try to market it.

At the annual strategic planning meeting, this idea was shared. Immediately, I looked at the mission statement and asked where in the mission statement of this pet service business did it allow for marketing software? My client readily recognized that this great idea could be a distraction rather than a great opportunity. Marketing software is totally different from providing pet services. Launching into this effort would only increase risk and divert assets away from the core business of the company. Wisely, my client dismissed this good idea as a distraction. This is an example of strategic boundaries.

Strategic boundaries are rooted in strategic plans and mission statements. King Solomon wrote:

> *He who works his land will have abundant food, but the one who chases fantasies will have his fill of poverty.*[23]

Solomon was articulating the importance of working one's land. Strategic planning is about defining one's land, which includes the boundaries of the land. The reverse is also true. If one does not define one's land, then one will chase fantasies.

Even Jesus was submitted to strategic boundaries. Note, for example, the following verses:

> *"Father, if you are willing, take this cup from me [Jesus]; yet not my will, but yours be done."*[24]
>
> *He [Jesus] answered, "I was sent only to the lost sheep of Israel."*[25]
>
> *Jesus gave them this answer: "I tell you the truth, the Son can do nothing by himself; he can do only what he sees his Father doing, because whatever the Father does the Son also does."*[26]
>
> *"I [Jesus] have brought you glory on earth by completing the work you gave me to do."*[27]

Jesus was not about doing His own will. Neither did He do everything that He could. He only did what the Father directed Him to do. He purposed and lived submitted to the strategic boundary of doing the will of the Father.

EVEN JESUS WAS SUBMITTED TO STRATEGIC BOUNDARIES.

Therefore, developing a strategic plan is not enough. One must also determine to have strategic boundaries to protect the plan and avoid distractions.

Strategic boundaries are necessary in every area of life, both individually and organizationally. The overriding boundary should be the same as for Jesus who only did the will of the Father.

For individuals, an example of strategic boundaries is prioritizing time to balance the various activities of life.

For organizations, an example of strategic boundaries is seeking God's

> **ORGANIZATIONS CAN ONLY BE EXCELLENT WHEN THEY FUNCTION UNDER THE CONSTRAINT OF WELL CONCEIVED STRATEGIC BOUNDARIES.**

will for the strategic plan of the organization and eliminating anything that impedes the faithful execution of the strategic plan. Another example is being faithful to follow the Golden Rule and other principles of the Bible.

Excellent organizations understand that strategic boundaries are not impediments but tools to facilitate excellent execution. Just as a railroad train can only run on rails and an airplane can only fly in the air, organizations can only be excellent when they function under the constraint of well conceived strategic boundaries.

Biblical Mandate

There is a bigger question regarding the strategic direction of organizations. The question is: Why does any organization exist? For many, the answer is to make money or create jobs. Is this all there is? If you accept a biblical worldview, the Bible provides an alternative answer.

The biblical mandate to Adam is the mandate to everyone individually and to every organization. The mandate gives each person and organization a reason for being: to multiply and to subdue the earth.

> *God blessed them and said to them, "Be fruitful and increase in number; fill the earth and subdue it."*[28]

Every organization is tasked by God to grow by multiplying and subduing. Multiplication implies reproduction. Subduing means overcoming obstacles. Organizations need to be continually improving in every way. It should be the objective of every organization to be on a never-ending search to find the best means and methods for improving its products and services. Jim Collins and Jerry Porras captured the sense of the divine mandate in the title of one of their chapters, "Good Enough Never Is."[29]

Organizations aligned with the divine mandate use strategic planning to build a culture of continuous improvement. In such cultures people are incessantly encouraged to grow personally. Ideas for improving all phases of the organization are eagerly embraced. When people noted the success of

J. Willard Marriott and encouraged him to rest; his reply was: "Oh, no. Got to keep going and do it better."[30]

Jack Welch, former CEO of GE, encouraged his executives to eliminate every impediment or boundary to finding the best ideas to solve every problem. He called this "boundaryless."[31] (This is different from strategic boundaries, which are necessary tools to protect strategic plans. Welch's term "boundaryless" means thinking outside the box with regard to problem solving.)

Both Marriott and Welch, perhaps unwittingly, understood the reality that their organizations must strategically embrace a culture that seeks the best methodologies for their organizations to grow and subdue. As a result, both built exemplary organizations.

Even companies based in countries, such as Japan, that largely do not embrace a biblical worldview, understand something of the divine mandate. For example, consider the comment by Tachi Kiuchi, managing director of Mitsubishi Electric Corporation: "My philosophy is, we don't run companies to earn profits. We earn profits to run companies. Our companies need meaning and purpose if they're to fit into the world, or why should they live at all?"[32]

Contrary to popular belief, organizations do not exist primarily to make money. Organizations exist to advance mankind's mastery of the physical world. Remember that organizations are simply groups of people who have joined together to accomplish a mission. That mission should be driven by a deep sense of purpose and meaning that transcends making money and creating jobs. Some researchers call it an "enduring purpose."[33]

Great enduring organizations have a profound sense that the reason for their being is to contribute to the good of the whole and to help make the world a better place. Dave Brown, former CEO of Lenscrafters, had an epiphany experience[34] with God in the early 1990s. Prior to that experience, he led Lenscrafters with the vision to be the biggest optical retailer in the galaxy and to make money. After his epiphany, he understood that God's purpose for Lenscrafters was to give the gift of sight and that money was not a primary driver but an indicator of God's favor and blessing for obeying Him.

Every excellent enduring organization must understand that it exists for a higher purpose or a greater good. A biblical worldview provides direction to organizations to glorify God by strategically growing and mastering the universe. As each organization seeks to glorify God through intentional and purposeful alignment with a biblical worldview, many wonderful things happen. There is provision for the organization that leads to jobs for workers, blessings to vendors, and profit to the shareholders.

Conclusion

Both individuals and organizations need to embrace the challenge to become aces. Aces acquire vision, clarify vision, and execute vision. Individually, aces are the building blocks for organizations that achieve excellence.

Every excellent organization has an adroitly developed strategic plan and mission statement that provides a definition of what the organization is to be about and the boundaries to keep the organization on course. Strategic plans are necessary but not sufficient for achieving excellence. There are many mediocre organizations that have strategic plans. Truly excellent organizations, however, build strategic plans and write well conceived mission statements based on the biblical thinking of its equally yoked senior leaders. When organizations execute strategic plans with impeccable excellence and tenacious accountability, world-class products and services are the fruit.

Points to Ponder

1. Are you an ace? Have you acquired a vision for your life? Are you engaged in clarifying your vision? Are you executing your vision?

2. Answer the same questions above for your church, family, business, and community.

3. Does your organization have a written strategic plan? If not, why not? If so, is the plan widely communicated, understood, and embraced by everyone in the organization? If your organization has a written strategic plan, is there accountability to the plan? Is every activity of your organization aligned with the strategic plan? Is everyone in the organization proactively supporting the strategic plan?

Notes

1. Proverbs 29:18 (KJV).
2. Esther 4:13–14.
3. Exodus 19:5.
4. Welch, *Jack:Straight from the Gut*, 209.
5. *Epiphanes*, 6 August 2003.
6. Hebrews 12:2–3.
7. Mary Duenwald, "More Americans Seeking Help for Depression," *New York Times*, 18 June 2003.
8. Proverbs 29:18.
9. Isaiah 46:11.
10. Proverbs 16:1.
11. Proverbs 16:9.
12. Proverbs 19:21.
13. Proverbs 16:1.
14. Proverbs 16:9.
15. Proverbs 19:21.
16. Proverbs 16:33.
17. Proverbs 21:30-31.
18. Proverbs 15:22.
19. Proverbs 20:18.
20. Proverbs 28:26.
21. Proverbs 21:5.
22. Proverbs 29:18 (KJV).
23. Proverbs 28:19.
24. Luke 22:42.
25. Matthew 15:24.
26. John 5:19.
27. John 17:4.
28. Genesis 1:28.
29. Collins and Porras, *Built to Last*, chapter 9.
30. Ibid., 185.
31. Welch, *Jack:Straight from the Gut*, 186.
32. Christine Canabou, "Hail Global Citizens," *Fast Company*, issue 78, January 2004, 59.
33. Collins and Porras, *Built to Last*, chapter 3.
34. "The Holy See," *Business Reform,* vol. 3, no. 4, p. 20.

Beyond Babel Model

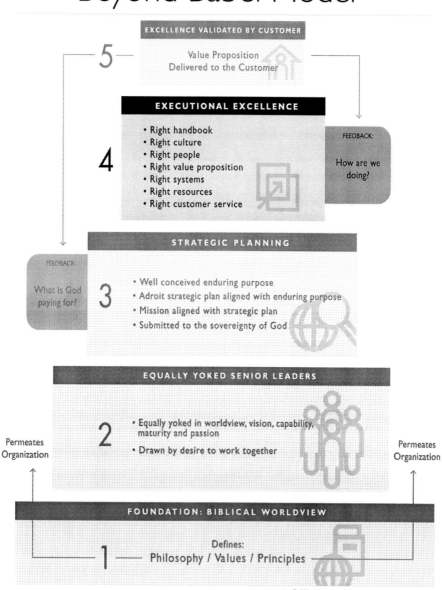

5 — EXCELLENCE VALIDATED BY CUSTOMER

Value Proposition
Delivered to the Customer

4 — EXECUTIONAL EXCELLENCE

- Right handbook
- Right culture
- Right people
- Right value proposition
- Right systems
- Right resources
- Right customer service

FEEDBACK:

How are we
doing?

3 — STRATEGIC PLANNING

FEEDBACK:

What is God
paying for?

- Well conceived enduring purpose
- Adroit strategic plan aligned with enduring purpose
- Mission aligned with strategic plan
- Submitted to the sovereignty of God

2 — EQUALLY YOKED SENIOR LEADERS

- Equally yoked in worldview, vision, capability, maturity and passion
- Drawn by desire to work together

Permeates
Organization

Permeates
Organization

1 — FOUNDATION: BIBLICAL WORLDVIEW

Defines:
Philosophy / Values / Principles

Executional Excellence

Most books purporting to articulate the principles that facilitate organizational excellence focus on the fourth step of the Beyond Babel Model: executional excellence. Clearly, it is the most practical step of the model.

However, sustained executional excellence cannot happen without well-conceived strategic plans developed by an equally yoked team of senior leaders operating based on a biblical philosophy. The philosophy must then be expressed in the operating principles and values that permeate the organization.

Executional excellence is an expression of the divine mandate.[1] Abraham Kuyper wrote: "The chief aim of all human effort remains what it was by virtue of our creation and before the

> "THE CHIEF AIM OF ALL HUMAN EFFORT REMAINS WHAT IT WAS BY VIRTUE OF OUR CREATION AND BEFORE THE FALL—NAMELY, DOMINION OVER NATURE."
>
> – ABRAHAM KUYPER

fall—namely, dominion over nature."[2] Dominion over nature means that every organization should reflect the glory of God on earth. This is done by multiplying and subduing creation.

Multiplying and subduing implies growth, development, and progress. In other words, every organization needs to be finding ways to deliver its products and services faster, better, and cheaper using biblical values and principles. By doing so, each organization will play its part in advancing the dominion of God's rule and reign on the earth.

Some may contend that the divine mandate was given to individuals but not to organizations. But what are organizations? Organizations are simply groups of people who have come together to accomplish a mission. Churches, schools, businesses, government agencies, and nonprofits are examples of organizations. Organizations are tools that individuals use to help them fulfill the divine mandate.

If this is indeed so, then by logical extension organizations are charged to fulfill the divine mandate just as individuals are. In fact, the divine mandate provides the reason and purpose for the existence of every individual and organization. All people individually and collectively are created to rule God's universe. People rule by two means, multiplying and subduing.

Multiplying implies growth and reproduction. Subduing implies gaining mastery over and bringing into submission. This is the process of human advancement. All research and development is an expression of man subduing God's creation in accordance with the divine mandate.

SIN IS SAND IN THE GEARS OF ORGANIZATIONS.

Challenging each organization's efforts to fulfill the divine mandate is the sin problem.[3] Sin is in the fabric of man and the physical world. The Bible teaches that the heavens declare the glory of God,[4] but sin impairs man's ability to see God's glory. This means that our sin blocks us from seeing God's philosophy, principles, and values. Furthermore, the entrance of sin appears to have impaired not only man but nature as well.[5] Therefore, sin becomes an impediment to man's efforts to obey the divine mandate. As Dennis Peacocke says, "Sin is sand in the gears"[6] of organizations.

The biblical solution to the sin problem is Jesus Christ.

*For Christ died for sins once for all, the righteous for the
unrighteous, to bring you to God...*[7]

By dealing with the sin problem, Jesus Christ opened the door for human beings to more fully do what they were created to do, namely, to fulfill the divine mandate. Because organizations are simply groups of people united to accomplish a mission, organizations must consider the reality of the nature of people as both spiritual and physical beings. This means that excellent organizations must embrace spiritual reality just as they embrace physical reality.

The biblical perspective is that spiritual reality precedes and defines physical reality.

Above all else, guard your heart, for it is the wellspring of life.[8]

This verse suggests that the heart, a metaphor for the spiritual dimension of each of us, is the root of our actions. For example, if we value truth and honesty, it will be reflected in our actions. Therefore, by recognizing the spiritual dimension of human existence as the foundation for actions, organizations can deal with the root issues or sins that impair organizational excellence.

One of my clients is in the staff augmentation business. Staff augmentation enables companies to supplement permanent staff on an "as needed" basis. Virtually every organization needs staff augmentation from time to time. Normally staff augmentation is short term, lasting just a few months. Occasionally, however, assignments can last for years. My client has one particular engagement that has lasted five years, an unusually long time in the staff augmentation business. Because of the long-term engagement, the person on this assignment decided to unilaterally renegotiate his contract.

Specifically, this individual made demands of my client that reflected arrogance and presumption, not to mention reneging on his contract. On the surface it appeared that the actions of the individual were motivated by money, but my client wisely recognized the real issue was something very intangible. The real issue was that the individual lacked character. If he would be so bold and brash with my client, what was he doing with the company to which he was assigned?

In reality, the demands by the individual were simply a wake-up call to my client. There is no way that executional excellence is going to be realized by someone who will not honor agreements and arrogantly makes demands based on self-interest. Clearly, this person is driven by the intangible force of sin in his heart that is manifested in the tangible world by demands rooted in greed and arrogance.

Excellent organizations recognize the reality of both the intangible or spiritual dimension and the tangible or physical dimension. And, to some degree, they also recognize the sin problem. Those that understand the solution to the sin problem have an enhanced opportunity to achieve organizational excellence. The more an organization walks in this understanding, the more potential it has for achieving excellence.

There are two levels of excellence. The first level is simply obeying principles of Scripture enabled only by common grace. For example, most people are able to be nice to others, which is a simple application of the Golden Rule. Clearly, this is better than not being nice. The second level is obeying the principles of Scripture enabled by the Holy Spirit. This level is only available to Christians. Obviously, this level should be superior to the first level. Christians empowered by the Holy Spirit should be operating in relationship with the God of Creation and in alignment with His philosophy, values, and principles. What would it be like for an organization to be composed of Christians empowered by the Holy Spirit? It would surely have to be world-class.

The starting point for building an excellent organization is an understanding of why God made man, namely, to rule His creation. Organizations are simply tools used by man to fulfill the mandate. Sin has complicated man's efforts to rule. People who live apart from the saving work of Christ can only be effective to the degree that they practice God's principles.

But even the best non-Christians who practice Godly principles are severely limited because they lack the Holy Spirit to guide and direct their lives. Those who embrace the saving work of Christ have the Holy Spirit to enable them to overcome sin in their lives. Therefore, in theory, Christians should have the greatest potential as workers. In practice, many Christians are no better than non-Christians because the Christians live no differently than the non-Christians. The objective for any management team seeking to build a great organization must be to find those workers who are empowered by the Holy Spirit *and* who are willing to practice God's principles.

The 7 Key Elements

Given this understanding, the remainder of this chapter focuses on practices that will facilitate excellence. Consider the following seven key elements in Diagram 5.

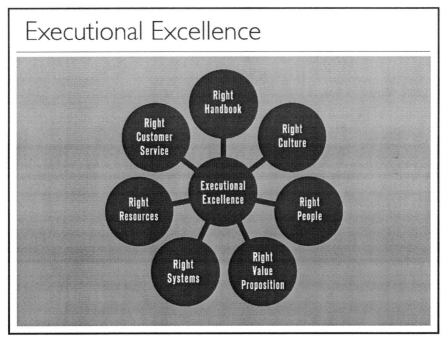

Diagram 5

Each of these elements is rooted in the philosophy, values, and principles of an organization. By practicing these seven elements, an organization will create a culture and operating paradigm that will be of enduring world-class status.

The philosophy, values, and principles provide the worldview of the organization. This is the most basic and critical element. Everything else in the organization is built on this worldview. The question is: What is the source or handbook for the philosophy, principles, and values?

The culture is a product of the operating practices embraced by the senior leaders. Into the culture, the right people are placed. That is, those who will align themselves with the strategic plan, worldview, and culture of the organization. Emanating from the right people is the value proposition, which though defined by the senior management must be adroitly executed by all workers. Supporting the workers are systems and resources that facilitate efficiency. World-class service is the necessary glue to see that the value proposition is impeccably supported.

1. Right Handbook

Most of us learned about organizational behavior either from business courses, books, or on the job training. Generally, all of these approaches adopt a pragmatic approach to discovering the philosophy, principles, and values that facilitate organizational excellence. A pragmatic approach assumes that there is no handbook that defines the philosophy, principles, and values that God intends for organizations to practice. For example, most people know that lying and cheating is not a good way to function. How did people learn this? Most learned it pragmatically through experience. If you lie to people, soon you will have no credibility. If you cheat on an exam, you might get caught and fail the exam.

For many today, pragmatism is an amoral ideology that embraces whatever works. In other words, a practice is viewed as acceptable if it is efficacious, with little to no consideration of morality. A common principle that is pragmatically embraced is that the end justifies the means. But what if the means are morally illicit?

Consider embezzlement. Some years ago my family business had a bookkeeper who was trusted implicitly. The bookkeeper got into a personal financial bind and needed money; however, she was too embarrassed to tell my dad, her boss. So she began embezzling. Randomly, she would write two checks to pay the same invoice. She would bring one of the checks to Dad for his signature and a week or so later, she would bring the duplicate check hoping that he would not remember signing the prior check. Then she would white out the name on the duplicate check and type in her own name. When the checks came back from the bank, she would change the names back. This worked for a long time, but finally the auditor noticed the white out and her name on the endorsement on the back of the checks.

Amoral pragmatism would suggest that embezzlement was okay because it worked for a long time. But in the end, amoral pragmatism does not work because it ignores the spiritual or intangible dimension of life and the reality that *"your sin will find you out."*[9]

Many today reject amoral pragmatism and embrace moral pragmatism. Searching the Web sites of the major publicly held companies, it is common to find a code of conduct. These are statements of values and principles. Interestingly, all the codes of conduct are essentially the same. They largely reflect a biblical value system. For example, chief among the values noted are integrity, honesty, trust, compassion, responsibility, excellence, truth, and justice. Though moral pragmatism is clearly better than amoral pragmatism and will bring a level of blessings and success, it still denies the existence of a handbook that defines the philosophy, principles, and values that facilitate organizational excellence.

As valuable as moral pragmatism is, it should not be the chief guide for defining organizational practice. A good example of moral pragmatism is seen in the story of King Saul.[10] Through the prophet Samuel, Saul was directed by the Lord to destroy all the Amalekites. Saul, however, in an example of pre-Darwinian thinking, only destroyed the weak and despised.

When confronted, Saul made an argument based on moral pragmatism. He indicated that he saved the best to sacrifice to the Lord. While his motive may sound noble, it was not in alignment with God's purpose. Therefore, God removed Saul and his heirs from ruling Israel. Moral pragmatism that is inconsistent with God's purpose does not lead to organizational practice that will be blessed.

The God of the Bible gave man the perfect handbook for organizational practice—the Bible. But, sadly, few view the Bible in this way. Why? If the God of the Bible created the universe, doesn't it logically follow that He would define the philosophy, principles, and values that He wants organizations to practice? This question is clearly rhetorical. My thesis is that the Bible is the handbook provided by God to define organizational practices that will enable organizations to do what they are supposed to do. Furthermore, organizations are simply tools for man to bring dominion to God's creation. This means that organizations should heuristically and pragmatically search out key principles of organizational excellence consistent with a biblical worldview.

> **THE BIBLE IS THE HANDBOOK PROVIDED BY GOD TO DEFINE ORGANIZATIONAL PRACTICES THAT WILL ENABLE ORGANIZATIONS TO DO WHAT THEY ARE SUPPOSED TO DO.**

In this philosophy of organizational excellence, amoral pragmatism is not acceptable since it lacks a moral filter to screen out illicit and sinful practices such as embezzlement. Although moral pragmatism is clearly superior to amoral pragmatism, it still suffers from an incomplete worldview. Moral pragmatists tend to accept a biblical value system, but the Bible provides more than values, it provides a worldview. Moral pragmatism must be elevated to the place of being submitted to a biblical perspective. Only then will pragmatism consistently lead to valid conclusions.

> **MORAL PRAGMATISM MUST BE ELEVATED TO THE PLACE OF BEING SUBMITTED TO A BIBLICAL PERSPECTIVE. ONLY THEN WILL PRAGMATISM CONSISTENTLY LEAD TO VALID CONCLUSIONS.**

Among Christians, a chief objection to the idea that the Bible is God's handbook for organizational practices is the assertion that the Bible does not speak to organizational matters. The argument is that the Bible is a book about redemption. Yes, the Bible contains the story of redemption and revelation about the Son of God. In fact, most of the Bible is dedicated to the story of redemption. Nevertheless, in the process of revealing the message of redemption, the Bible reveals philosophy, values, and principles that can be used to guide organizations. For example, consider the principle of firstfruits.

Honor the LORD with your wealth, with the firstfruits of all your crops; then your barns will be filled to overflowing, and your vats will brim over with new wine.[11]

This principle is rooted in the reality that God is the provider. Seeds are planted by the farmer, but the germination and growth of the seed is the blessing of God. There is no guarantee that the farmer's work will bear fruit. The mystery of this process is that people have a role to play in events, but can't control events.

The metaphor can be applied in every area of life. For example, consider the sales process. Like the diligent farmer, a salesperson sows seeds with customers by providing a cogent and compelling case for the salesperson's product or service. In an unregulated society where free enterprise is allowed to operate, the decision to buy is not the salesperson's, it is the customer's. Therefore, when the salesperson receives an order, the proper attitude should be gratitude expressed to the Lord for the favor of the business—the increase of the work of his hands. Gratitude is properly expressed to God by honoring Him with the firstfruits. The principle of firstfruits means that giving to the Lord is a priority.

Consider the principle of advisers:

Plans fail for lack of counsel, but with many advisers they succeed.[12]

The principle of advisers is rooted in the reality that every person is limited. No human is omniscient. Each of us has different perspectives, understanding, and wisdom. Furthermore, we all tend to be deceived about ourselves. To solve a vexing conundrum or question, wise people tap into the power of advisers—people with C4.

The above principles and many more are contained in the Bible. The Bible is God's revelation to His creation and speaks to all of life—spiritual and physical. It provides us with the reason for our being, namely, to rule God's physical universe and to glorify God. Since man has been given that task, does it not follow that God would reveal the means and methods for executing the task? Therefore, the Bible should be viewed as a source of philosophy, principles, and values that will enable man to fully express the glory of God as man rules God's creation. If one rejects the Bible as the handbook for organizational practice, one is left with moral pragmatism as the best alternative.

Organizations can achieve a level of excellence using moral pragmatism. Southwest Airlines is a great example. Faithfully following the Golden Rule,[13] Southwest is perennially recognized as the best airline in the United States. But if my thesis is correct, Southwest Airlines could achieve another level of excellence if it adopted the entire Bible as its handbook for organizational practice.

Whether organizations understand it or not, embracing biblical principles and values facilitates organizational excellence and prosperity. Many of these principles and practices can be pragmatically learned. But ultimately the standard against which all pragmatic learning must be measured is the Bible.

2. Right Culture

The culture of every organization is the product of the organization's worldview that is defined by senior management. Southwest Airlines values their workers; the culture is known for practicing the Golden Rule—simply treating others the way that you want to be treated. This one principle is so strong at Southwest that it is the dominant driver of the culture.

EMC is known for its world-class service.[14] In a time when most organizations seek to deflect responsibility for problems, EMC does the opposite. EMC's culture is so service-oriented that when a customer has a problem, EMC owns the problem until it can be proven that the problem belongs to someone else. Engineers, who in most companies are shielded from customer service, are physically co-located with the customer service staff. The service department is not a profit center since placing profit goals on the department would be counterproductive to the culture of world-class service.

The culture of an organization defines the environment of the organization. Some organizations promote open communication while others don't. Some organizations manage by serving while others manage by intimidation. Some organizations promote working hard while others promote working smart. Some organizations value employee ideas while others want rigid adherence to accepted practices. Each of these different organizational qualities defines a different organizational culture.

One of my clients is a ministry to the homeless. To help support the ministry, the organization has a business operation. The person in charge of the business operation is a very capable young man. I received a call one day from this young man. The ministry was struggling financially because of the slow economy that impacted both the business activities and the charitable contributions. The CEO of the ministry decided that the senior leaders needed to reduce their salaries and indicated that a meeting would be called to discuss the matter.

The meeting was never called and the CEO made the changes he deemed appropriate. Needless to say, the manager of the business operation was quite upset, and rightfully so, because the CEO had violated the principle of clear agreements.[15] He made a commitment and failed to honor his commitment. Such conflicts divert emotional and physical energy that could be devoted to useful work. This type of culture is discouraging and counterproductive.

Excellent organizations are known to have cultures that value people and therefore promote employee performance. These cultures typically allow people to "fall forward," meaning that when people make mistakes, the organization encourages them to learn from their mistakes. Cultures that value people embrace meritocracy. Such cultures breed extraordinary acts by workers.

> **CULTURES THAT VALUE PEOPLE EMBRACE MERITOCRACY. SUCH CULTURES BREED EXTRAORDINARY ACTS BY WORKERS.**

On one occasion, the gratitude of the workers of Delta Airlines toward management overflowed. The workers pooled their resources and bought a new airplane for the company. When R. G. LeTourneau's company was on the brink of bankruptcy, his workers bought the necessary tools and equipment to allow the company to operate if the company was forced into bankruptcy. What prompts workers to do such amazing things?

The answer is the right culture. The right culture empowers and encourages workers. The right culture releases people to be who they are called and destined to be. The right culture promotes excellence that leads to prosperity. The right culture is the product of alignment with biblical principles and practices.

3. Right People

As important as the right culture is, it isn't sufficient to produce organizational excellence. What must be coupled to a culture rooted in biblical reality are the right people. Every organization must have people to manage and execute the organization's mission. So how does an organization find the right people? The answer: equal yoking and C4.

The principles of equal yoking and C4 were explained in a prior chapter. Equal yoking is a principle of balance. For a yoked system to produce maximum efficiency, those pulling the load must be pulling equally. Any person who fails to pull his or her load creates an unequal yoking situation that requires compensation from the other members of the organization. The more energy that is diverted to compensating for unequal yoking, the less efficient a system will be.

The criterion for determining equal yoking is C4: calling, character, capability, and commissioning. A person who is called to do a certain activity has a passion for it. Character refers to a person's values and principles, which are the product of the person's worldview. Alignment between the worldview of the organization and the individuals in the organization is essential to minimize conflicts in philosophy and practices. Capability reflects a person's developed skill, ability, training, experience, and education. Commissioning is a measure of external validation that a person has received and the release that the organization provides to facilitate the person's performance.

> **THE MORE ENERGY THAT IS DIVERTED TO COMPENSATING FOR UNEQUAL YOKING, THE LESS EFFICIENT A SYSTEM WILL BE.**

When an organization embraces the C4 principle, there is recognition that people are not fungible. In other words, for each job there is the right person. When there is a job opening, the management team of the organization should not be looking for a person to fill the job. They need to be looking for the right person. The right person will have C4 to do that job and therefore will be equally yoked to the organization.

Of the C4 components, character is perhaps the hardest to change. George Barna's research on worldview reveals that the worldview of each person is defined or hardwired—to use an electrical metaphor—by the age of thirteen.[16] Some may stray from their worldview for a time, but in the end they will return. King Solomon taught this truth.[17] This means that a person's family of origin can provide an important clue as to the character that can be expected from that person.

A new field of study called "emotional inefficient"[18] is emerging. Researchers have discovered that dysfunctional childhood behavior patterns are brought into the workplace, creating inefficiencies. For example, a manager inappropriately explodes when teased by a subordinate. The root of this behavior is a lack of training as a child regarding appropriate emotional responses.

Another example is a company with an oppressive climate; every worker feels that his or her efforts are never enough. The root issue is the owner's family of origin in which no one ever could do enough. A two-year study by one researcher concluded that 20 to 50 percent of workers' time is wasted because of emotional inefficiencies.[19] Furthermore, the study also concluded that people tend to be hired based on capability and terminated based on personality or character issues.

Since sin is systemic in humanity, it is not surprising that dysfunctional childhood behavior would be carried into adult life. The solution to emotional inefficiency is to embrace a biblical worldview that begins with accepting Christ as Savior and to purpose to live for Him. Many people profess to have accepted Christ, but few seem to walk in that reality. This means that few people really have a biblical worldview.

According to research by George Barna, only 4 percent of Americans have a biblical worldview.[20] This reality presents a major obstacle to building equally yoked organizations. It also means there is a major opportunity. Since few people have a biblical worldview, there are few organizations that are equally yoked. Hence, there are few organizations that deliver truly excellent products and services.

Some will contend that ethics is sufficient to assess character. While ethics is important, it is only one indicator of a person's character. Another, and perhaps a more important indicator of character, is how a person responds to God's special revelation, the Bible. People who reject God's law have a big problem. Namely, their communication with God is impaired. Note what Solomon said:

> *If anyone turns a deaf ear to the law, even his prayers are detestable.*[21]

The apostle Peter noted what happens to a husband's prayer life when he fails to properly treat his wife:

> *Husbands, in the same way be considerate as you live with your wives, and treat them with respect as the weaker part-ner and as heirs with you of the gracious gift of life, so that nothing will hinder your prayers.*[22]

These texts suggest that people who do not properly respond to God's revelation in the Bible cannot expect their prayers to be heard. This is amazing. If this is true, is it wise to hire someone whose prayers are hindered?

This is a challenging concept, because we are accustomed to assuming that God has little to do with organizational activities. Whether wittingly or not, we assume that God is mainly interested in spiritual matters and, therefore, physical matters are of little concern to Him. As a result of this mind-set, it is easy for us to dismiss a person's private life as irrelevant to employment.

A great illustration of this false thinking was the impeachment of former President Clinton. Though he was clearly guilty of illicit sexual activities and lying, he was not removed from office. Why? Because Congress, and the American people, believed that a person's lack of character did not impair his ability to make wise public policy decisions. As a result, America had a president who did not have the ear of God. Now, that is scary. Why would any organization want to hire or elect people who do not have the ear of God? In the words of the *Star Trek* character, Mr. Spock, it is not logical.

When an organization has the right people, the organization will be running on all eight cylinders, to use an automobile metaphor. There will be minimal conflict since there will be worldview alignment within the organization. Everyone in the organization will be working in concert to accomplish the organization's mission. Excellent products and services will be the fruit of this reality.

WHY WOULD ANY ORGANIZATION WANT TO HIRE OR ELECT PEOPLE WHO DO NOT HAVE THE EAR OF GOD?

4. Right Value Proposition

Who wants to buy mediocre products and services? This may seem like a ludicrous question, but in reality it is a sobering question. Daily we make decisions, many times unwittingly, assessing quality and convenience against price. In other words, customers are always assessing the quality and convenience (value) received in return for the price paid. Each organization providing products and services must then determine its value proposition. Why would any customer value its products? Therefore, since it is axiomatic that each organization wants its customers to use its products, the right products are those that its customers value. Every organization must define and communicate its value proposition.

As simplistic as this concept may seem, finding and executing the right value proposition is difficult for any organization. This is one of the main reasons that 80 percent of all new business ventures fail. Consider, for example, the United States Postal Service (USPS). For years, the USPS has functioned as a quasi-monopoly. Their value proposition over the past few decades seems to be to deliver mail and packages with minimal customer service and to increase rates as quickly as possible because the customers don't have many other options.

With the explosive growth of e-mail, electronic bill paying, and alternative package delivery, the USPS's old value proposition is no longer viable. To compete with private enterprise that is motivated to deliver an excellent value proposition, the USPS must find a competitive value proposition. However, changing quasi-monopolies is vexing. In fact, it is so difficult that Congress even considered taxing e-mail and giving the proceeds to the USPS.

If the USPS were a private enterprise, it would probably be bankrupt. On the other hand, FedEx and UPS are working hard to improve their respective value propositions. Given the quality of the competition, the USPS may, in the end, not succeed in developing a competitive value proposition without considerable government assistance.

Developing a good value proposition is just the beginning. Organizations must be able to communicate their value proposition. A wonderful technique for doing this is called branding. According to Stan Richards and David Culp, "a brand is a promise … Branding, as a business discipline, is the process of coming to a conviction about the expectations you want established, understanding every mechanism that affects those expectations, and managing those mechanisms to deliver a consistent, positive promise at every point of contact."[23]

Branding gives an organization notoriety and recognition. There is perhaps no brand more readily recognized than that of Neiman Marcus. The Neiman Marcus brand stands for quality merchandise worldwide. Neiman's reputation is so strong that even a box or bag with the Neiman Marcus name is valued. Why? Because people assume that within the box or bag is something from Neiman Marcus, and everything from Neiman Marcus is top quality.

Biblically, the basis for branding can be found in texts such as Proverbs 22:1:

A good name is more desirable than great riches;
to be esteemed is better than silver or gold.

The value of a good name or reputation cannot be denominated in hard currency. A person's or an organization's character is embodied in their name or brand. The one quality of every person or organization that is totally within the purview of the person or organization is found in that person's or organization's principles and values.

Great people and great organizations understand the power of making good choices about their principles and values so that they enjoy a good reputation. Every excellent organization works hard to develop a brand that embodies its reputation. Nordstrom is known for service. Wal-Mart's value proposition is low price. Walgreen offers convenience. Whatever an organization's value proposition, the proposition must be valued by those who use the products of the organization. In this way and only in this way does an organization offer the right products.

5. Right Systems

Some years ago, a major organization used the branding tag line "the system is the solution"—a clever saying that conveys an important reality. The purpose of systems is to support each organization's value proposition as efficiently as possible. This is done by facilitating work and establishing boundaries.

The Right Systems Facilitate Work

Facilitating work is simply using systems to minimize human involvement in routine, mundane matters. Systems are great tools for processing orders, filling orders, scheduling projects, solving mathematical problems, performing accounting functions, processing words and thoughts, developing presentations, storing and manipulating data, and so forth. However, any function requiring a personal touch, such as customer service, is generally best performed by the right people.

The Right Systems Establish Boundaries

A key role for systems is to establish boundaries. Establishing boundaries is about keeping the organization on course. Every organization will have distractions—great opportunities that don't really fit the value proposition. Amazon.com is building a seminal Web site for consumer products. The site is rife with links to other sites that are Amazon partners. These partners are strategically selected to fill in gaps in Amazon's product offering.

From the beginning, Amazon knew that to be the industry leader, it had to have a Web site that was difficult to duplicate. Therefore, during the early years, profit was sacrificed so that all available resources could be invested in building the Web site. The site is now a key system that guides, directs, and protects Amazon's business. Amazon's Web site is so intelligent that it can make suggestions, track orders, send e-cards with music, remember key customer dates, remember customers' wishes, and communicate those wishes. All of this highly sophisticated automation is about keeping Amazon on course to become the dominant company selling consumer products over the Internet.

Another strategic boundary provided by systems is sin management. Sin management is the systematic protection of an organization and its stakeholders from the sins of others, such as theft. The whole reason for personal identification numbers (PINs) is sin management. Audits of various types are intended to provide assurance to all stakeholders that the various activities of the organization are being conducted appropriately. Passwords and security codes are intended to provide further protection from industrial espionage, thieves, hackers, and terrorists.

Sadly, the reality of sin is that it is all about us and affects all of us. According to the Bible, every human being without Jesus Christ is in bondage to sin.[24] It would be wonderful if organizations could rely on workers, customers, and vendors to always act appropriately, but alas, this is not reality. During the days of King Josiah, the temple was rebuilt. It was said of those who were doing the work:

> *They did not require an accounting from those to whom they gave the money to pay the workers, because they acted with complete honesty.*[25]

How wonderful it would be if this was always true in organizations today, but it isn't. In my own experience, I witnessed embezzlement by a bookkeeper and theft by a warehouseman. Both of these people were longtime, trusted, and able workers who allowed temptation to master them. In the end, they were caught by the systems. The right systems can be effective in helping organizations establish a strategic boundary to protect against sin.

Though sin management is not the solution for the sin problem, it is a necessary reality for people to relate and do business in a world where sin is systemic. The only solution for sin is the work of Christ at the Cross. But even the people who embrace Christ struggle with sin through what the Bible calls the flesh.[26] Walking out one's salvation is not easy and everyone on the journey will fail from time to time. Thankfully, the full devastation of sin is restrained by means of God's common grace.

6. Right Resources

By resources, I mean primarily financial resources. But the term also includes people, technology, systems, facilities, and other assets.

The biggest issue relative to the right resources is perspective. It is typical to hear people say they would do something *if* they had the resources. From a biblical worldview, this is illogical. God, as the Creator of the universe, has access to all resources. He created everything out of nothing.[27] If God wants to do something, resources are not a problem. Consider the words of the prophet Isaiah:

> *I make known the end from the beginning, from ancient times, what is still to come. I say: My purpose will stand, and I will do all that I please. From the east I summon a bird of prey; from a far-off land, a man to fulfill my purpose. What I have said, that will I bring about; what I have planned, that will I do.*[28]

A clue to finding what a person or organization should be doing is to take inventory. Consider the assets, relationships, understanding, and opportunities. This inventory is an indication as to what God wants an individual or organization to do.

Given that resources are not an issue, here are some principles to consider relative to the right resources:

The first principle is expressed in Luke 14:28:

> *Suppose one of you wants to build a tower. Will he not first sit down and estimate the cost to see if he has enough money to complete it?*

This is the principle of counting the cost. Every organization must assess the cost to exist and execute its strategic plan. The cost is not only financial but also includes other resources such as people, technology, systems, and facilities. The right resources are, therefore, the combination of all assets required to efficiently execute the strategic plan. Excess resources do not produce additional return. Likewise, if an organization has inadequate resources, it will not be able to

IF GOD WANTS TO DO SOMETHING, RESOURCES ARE NOT A PROBLEM.

execute its mission with excellence. This begs the question of whether or not the organization has the right strategic plan or whether the organization should even exist.

The second principle is expressed in Matthew 6:33:

But seek first his kingdom and his righteousness, and all these things will be given to you as well.

"Seek first his kingdom and his righteousness" provides each human with a divine directive. Our focus is to seek God's rule and reign in accordance with His standard of rightness (values and principles). The immediate context of this verse implies that the phrase "all these things" refers to the daily needs of all humans: food, clothing, and shelter. Therefore, the verse is conveying the principle that if we seek to align our lives with God and therefore do His will, that He will take care of our needs. Regarding this principle, Dennis Peacocke says, "God pays for what He orders."[29]

The challenge for every organization is to discern what God is funding. All too frequently, organizations act presumptuously and embark on activities with inadequate resources or presumptuously take on debt. Either route can be devastating.

It requires incredible patience and trust in God to wait until the resources are in place before embarking on a project. Perhaps a lack of patience and faith are key reasons that most new ventures fail. On the other hand, when God wants to do something, resources are not a problem. Since God is the Creator of the universe, resources are never a problem for Him. Therefore in a very real sense, there is no such thing as a resource problem. When an organization perceives that there is a resource problem, the management of the organization is simply revealing that they have not discovered what God is funding.

GOD PAYS FOR WHAT HE ORDERS.

Since the sovereign God of the universe is about doing His will,[30] does it not follow that an organization's resources and activities will be congruent? When an organization correlates its activities with its resources, it discovers the right resources to do what God has called the organization to do.

7. Right Customer Service

What is "right customer service"? Right customer service is built on the Golden Rule:

Do to others as you would have them do to you.[31]

The Golden Rule is about treating others the way that you would want to be treated if the roles were reversed. More often than not, the customer service offered by organizations is very self-serving. Consider, for example, my experience buying a new cell phone.

Unsatisfied with her cell phone, my wife wanted a new, and hopefully improved, phone. A nearby phone store operated by my service provider seemed to be the logical venue for conducting this business. Upon arriving at the store, I was met by a long line of people waiting for service. Being a rather impatient type, I decided to come back later when it was not so busy. Much to my chagrin, subsequent visits did nothing to improve my position. I simply had to take a number and wait. The wait was approximately thirty minutes.

While standing (not sitting) in line, we (my wife had accompanied me this time) noticed a lady walk into the store. She ignored the line and in a few minutes an eager salesperson waited on her. My wife, determined to know what was going on, discovered that the lady was not an existing customer, but a potential customer. I was in a line for existing customers. So what was the message? Customers stand in line for service. After all, the company already gets checks each month from its customers. But potential customers get special treatment. However, once the company has you signed up for that monthly check, then you become a customer and must wait in line for customer service.

Have you noticed that many companies provide toll free numbers and plenty of sales representatives to minimize wait times if you wish to buy a product or service? Customers needing support, however, are treated as second-class citizens. They have the privilege of paying their own long distance charges to call the company and then enjoy the interminable wait for the support person.

Is this customer service or as some call it today, "customer care"? If an organization really cares about its customers, why would it treat them so

WHEN ORGANIZATIONS HAVE THE RIGHT PEOPLE WITH A HEART TO PRACTICE THE GOLDEN RULE, INCREDIBLE SERVICE HAPPENS.

poorly? Shouldn't customers be treated with genuine care and gratitude? If so, should not the operating practices of organizations reward customers? Clearly, most agree with the need to honor customers. However, when it comes to spending the time, money, and resources to express this sentiment, few organizations are willing to pay the price.

On the other hand, when organizations have the right people with a heart to practice the Golden Rule, incredible service happens. Consider the following examples cited in a *Newsweek Online* interview with Herb Kelleher, chairman of Southwest Airlines.

A guy calls our (Southwest Airlines) Dallas reservation center from St. Louis, and he tells the reservation agent that TWA has canceled its flight out of DFW (Dallas–Fort Worth airport) to St. Louis on which his 85-year-old mother was supposed to fly, and that he's very concerned about her coming over to Love Field and having to make an intermediate connection in Tulsa. So the reservation agent says: I'm going to be off in five minutes. I'll pick her up at DFW, drive her to Love Field, and fly with her to St. Louis to make sure that she gets there O.K.[32]

A guy has a heart attack at Love Field. He goes to the hospital. Our ticket agent stays there all night, calling his wife to let her know how he's doing. I got a letter from a passenger on another airline who said: Herb, I couldn't believe it. I had gotten off the airline, went to the parking lot, and I had a flat tire. And one of your people came along and changed the tire for me, and I said: You know I didn't fly Southwest Airlines. He said: I don't care. That has nothing to do with whether you fly Southwest Airlines. That's the kind of folks that we want.[33]

The right customer service is rooted in not only the culture of the organization but also in the people. Southwest Airlines goes the extra mile to find the right people who, on their own, practice the Golden Rule. And because of this, Southwest Airlines has the lowest complaint record of any airline.[34]

Invariably when providing customer service based on the Golden Rule, an organization will encounter customers, vendors, and others who don't share the organization's values. The Golden Rule compels one to resist the temptation to compromise. Revenge is a temptation for every human that is mistreated. However, revenge does not lead to blessing. What helps us in trying situations where people are abusing the organization and/or the people in the organization is to remember that God is in charge:

> *Do not take revenge, my friends, but leave room for God's wrath, for it is written: "It is mine to avenge; I will repay," says the Lord.*[35]

In dealing with customers, vendors, and others who abuse the goodwill of the organization, however, it is reasonable to set boundaries to protect the organization. But in so doing, always keep in mind to err on the side of going the extra mile. For years, Wal-Mart allowed customers to return any product for a full refund, regardless of the reason or product condition or time of ownership. As a result some customers abused this policy by using the products for personal purposes and, when through with the product, returned it for full credit. In essence, the product was used rent-free. As a result, Wal-Mart would return perfectly good but used products to vendors for full credit. The vendors were being abused. Gradually, Wal-Mart is changing this policy. While it is still very generous with customer returns, it now requires valid reasons for returns. This is an appropriate boundary that is consistent with practicing the Golden Rule.

Conclusion

Since the common ingredient of every organization is people, executional excellence by organizations begins by understanding the basic nature of people, which is rooted in sin, and God's solution, namely, the work of Jesus Christ on the cross. Coupled to this reality is the right handbook

> **ORGANIZATIONAL UTOPIA HAPPENS WHEN PEOPLE WALK IN A BIBLICAL WORLDVIEW IN THE POWER OF THE HOLY SPIRIT DOING WHAT GOD HAS ORDAINED THE ORGANIZATION TO DO.**

of organizational behavior, the Bible. The Bible provides the worldview (philosophy, principles, and values) needed to adroitly execute the organization's strategic plan. In addition, the divine mandate of Genesis 1:26–28 charges man with the responsibility to research and subdue the physical universe, not using amoral pragmatism but moral pragmatism submitted to a biblical worldview. This is the way that God intended His creation to operate.

With this understanding, each excellent organization develops the right value proposition and finds the right people to facilitate the execution of its strategic plan. Understanding that God is sovereignly in control enables organizations to seek to align their activities and resources with God's will. Alignment with His will is the only strategy that is enduringly successful.

Finally, the right systems and the right customer service enable efficient execution. Organizational utopia happens when people walk in a biblical worldview in the power of the Holy Spirit doing what God has ordained the organization to do.

The external indicators of organizational excellence are products that are faster, better, and cheaper than those of competing organizations and world-class service. Excellent organizations are built on a solid foundation and display a high level of focus. They will find and utilize the best operational practices and will enjoy excellent reputations.

Points to Ponder

1. Describe the philosophy of your organization.

2. List the five most important values of your organization. Correlate each of these values to specific principles practiced by your organization.

3. Assess your organization against the seven keys to organizational excellence.

    Right handbook

    Right culture

    Right people

    Right value proposition

    Right systems

    Right resources

    Right customer service

Notes

1. Genesis 1:26–28.

2. Abraham Kuyper, *Christianity: A Total World and Life System* (UK: Gilliland Press, 1996), 56.

3. Genesis 3.

4. Psalms 19.

5. Romans 8:22–23.

6. Private communication.

7. 1 Peter 3:18.

8. Proverbs 4:23.

9. Numbers 32:23.

10. 1 Samuel 15.

11. Proverbs 3:9–10.

12. Proverbs 15:22.

13. Matthew 7:12.

14. Paul C. Judge, "Customer Service: EMC Corp.," *Fast Company*, issue 47, June 2001, 138.

15. Matthew 5:37.

16. "Research Shows That Spiritual Maturity Process Should Start at a Young Age," http://www.barna.org, 17 October 2003.

17. Proverbs 22:6.

18. Michelle Conlin, "I Am a Bad Boss? Blame Dad," *BusinessWeek Online*, 10 May 2004.

19. Ibid.

20. "A Biblical Worldview Has a Radical Effect on a Person's Life," http://www.barna.org, 1 December 2003.

21. Proverbs 28:9.

22. 1 Peter 3:7.

23. Stan Richards and David Culp, *The Peaceable Kingdom* (NY: John Wiley & Sons, 2001), 206–207.

24. Romans 3:23.

25. 2 Kings 12:15.

26. Romans 7 (especially vs. 25).

27. Genesis 1

28. Isaiah 46:10–11.

29. Dennis Peacocke, *Doing Business God's Way*, chapter 6.

30. Isaiah 46:11.

31. Luke 6:31.

32. "Herb Kelleher on the Record, part 3," *Business Week Online*, 24 December 2003.

33. Ibid.

34. Ibid.

35. Romans 12:19.

Beyond Babel Model

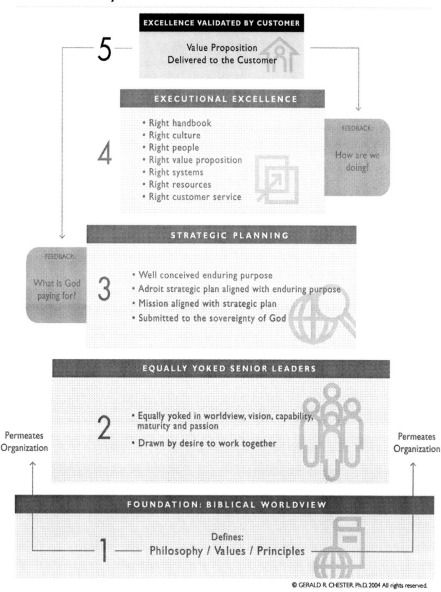

EXCELLENCE VALIDATED BY CUSTOMER

5 .... Value Proposition
Delivered to the Customer

EXECUTIONAL EXCELLENCE

4
- Right handbook
- Right culture
- Right people
- Right value proposition
- Right systems
- Right resources
- Right customer service

FEEDBACK:
How are we doing?

STRATEGIC PLANNING

FEEDBACK:
What is God paying for?

3
- Well conceived enduring purpose
- Adroit strategic plan aligned with enduring purpose
- Mission aligned with strategic plan
- Submitted to the sovereignty of God

EQUALLY YOKED SENIOR LEADERS

2
- Equally yoked in worldview, vision, capability, maturity and passion
- Drawn by desire to work together

Permeates Organization

Permeates Organization

FOUNDATION: BIBLICAL WORLDVIEW

1 —— Defines:
Philosophy / Values / Principles

Excellence Validated by the Customer: The Ultimate Test

The CEO of a restaurant chain was interviewed by a reporter. In the course of the interview, the reporter commented that the price points of his company's food offerings were below the competition's. The CEO agreed and added that he believed customers viewed his offerings as a superior value proposition. No basis for this assertion was offered by either the CEO or the reporter. The CEO's comment was based on the CEO's perception. How do I know? It's really quite simple. Most likely, if the CEO had any credible research to support his position, he would have readily cited it. What this CEO revealed is common Level 4 thinking. Level 4 leaders tend to believe what they want to believe even without evidence to support it. In my experience, it is the rare CEO who submits his or her perspective to the scrutiny of customers. If my observations are more than anecdotal, there are few Level 5 CEOs; few CEOs really know their customers' perception of their value proposition. Isn't it logical that the people buying an organization's products would be in the best position to render a judgment on the value proposition?

The fifth and final step of the Beyond Babel Model is customer validation of the product or, as scholars say, value proposition. The biblical principle that speaks to the issue of validation of products is stated by Solomon in Proverbs 27:2:

> *Let another praise you, and not your own mouth; someone*
> *else, and not your own lips.*

Praise from one's own lips is never credible. No one can self-validate. Yet it is common for leaders to praise their organizations and to put a positive spin on everything. Typically, this action is justified as being necessary to keep a positive light on the organization. But all too often this positive spin is just a cover for an unwillingness to face truth and reality.

One of the limitations of every human being is that he or she doesn't see himself or herself as accurately as others do. Our self-perception is fundamentally and inherently incomplete and defective. Frequently others seek to communicate the truth to us, but we refuse to receive it. We choose rather to embrace denial and deception. The truth of this concept was expressed by Jesus when He spoke the following words:

NO ONE CAN SELF-VALIDATE.

> *How can you say to your brother, "Let me take the speck out*
> *of your eye," when all the time there is a plank in your own*
> *eye? You hypocrite, first take the plank out of your own eye,*
> *and then you will see clearly to remove the speck from your*
> *brother's eye.*[1]

These verses suggest that each of us has a metaphorical plank in our eye that needs to be removed for us to be able to see clearly. The question is: What is the plank? I suggest that the plank is sin. Sin is anything that is inconsistent with God's righteousness, because anything inconsistent with God's righteousness blocks our ability to perceive truth and reality accurately.

In 1987, Johnson & Johnson acquired the patent to the stent. In 1994, the FDA granted approval to use the stent for coronary conditions. The first version of the stent was released in 1995 and implanted in more than one hundred thousand people. Also in 1995, J&J acquired an angioplasty balloon company, which enabled J&J to package a complete angioplasty unit. By 1997, J&J's market share was 95 percent. Its gross margin on the stent package was 80 percent. Its stent, however, had problems. There was only one size. The stent was not flexible and it was difficult to see by X-ray. Also, it was expensive. Medical doctors expressed their concerns to J&J, but to no avail.

Competition responded to the doctors. In 1998, Guidant introduced a multi-stent unit that addressed many of the problems of J&J's unit. Consequently, it was well received by the medical community, which caused J&J's market share to drop from 95 percent to less than 30 percent. J&J's explanation was that they had a patent, so why bother with a second generation stent? [2] This attitude revealed a large plank in the eye of J&J that blocked its ability to see truth and reality. The truth was that the patent meant little if someone could develop a better stent that didn't violate the patent. So what was the plank? The plank was the sin of resting on past laurels and ignoring the need to always try to improve.

The biblical principle of growth and continuous improvement is articulated in the divine mandate as follows:

> *God blessed them and said to them, "Be fruitful and increase in number; fill the earth and subdue it. Rule over the fish of the sea and the birds of the air and over every living creature that moves on the ground."* [3]

The key word is *subdue*. *Subdue* means "to master." To gain mastery over something requires continuous improvement since there is no end of the efforts to master. By resting on their laurels, J&J was deceived into thinking their market position was secure. The price of this deception was blindness regarding the truth and reality about the stent market.

Sydney Finkelstein gives us some insight into some of the planks of smart but not Level 5 executives. He writes that, contrary to popular belief, executive failure is rooted in intangible not tangible issues. The common cause of executive failure, as viewed by many, is rooted in tangible issues, such as lack of resources, poor planning, and wrong people. Dr. Finkelstein contends that these tangible effects are symptoms, not root issues. He argues that the foundation of an individual's behavior is that person's intangible belief system or worldview. The intangible belief system is manifested tangibly in the behavior, actions, and choices of an individual. The key planks, or sin, in the eye of failed executives are pride, self-centeredness, deception, and fear. Dr. Finkelstein's thesis is that there are seven habits that explain the failure of spectacularly unsuccessful people:[4]

1. They see themselves and their companies as dominating their environments.

2. They identify so completely with the company that there is no clear boundary between their personal interests and their corporation's interests.

3. They think they have all the answers.

4. They ruthlessly eliminate anyone who isn't 100 percent behind them.

5. They are consummate company spokespersons, obsessed with the company image.

6. They underestimate major obstacles.

7. They stubbornly rely on what worked for them in the past.

Habits 1, 3, 5, and 6 are rooted in pride and self-deception. The antidote to pride and deception is humility. Habit 2 compromises the good of the organization with the executive's personal agenda, which is highly self-centered. The antidote to self-centeredness is selflessness. Habits 4 and 7 are rooted in fear. The antidote to fear is trust. Very smart people can have big planks and, therefore, make very big mistakes. In fact, every human being can and does display these seven characteristics or planks from time to time. To avoid doing so would require great maturity.

Who among us walks in selfless humility and trust every moment? No one does. We all are subject to these sins and their consequences. One of the chief consequences is deception that blocks one's ability to accurately see truth and reality. King Solomon warned against deception when he said:

He who trusts in himself is a fool, but he who walks in wisdom is kept safe.[5]

Any person who desires to walk in wisdom will seek input from others to validate his or her self-perspective. In the case of an organization's value proposition, the customers who purchase the value proposition are in the best position to provide perspective on the organization if they have C4 to render such input.

ANY PERSON WHO DESIRES TO WALK IN WISDOM WILL SEEK INPUT FROM OTHERS.

The Importance of C4 Customers

C4 is the basic qualification criterion for any job. This is also true of the job of validating the quality of an organization's value proposition. When obtaining such input, organizations would be wise to qualify the input, not for the purpose of screening negative input, but for the purpose of hearing an unbiased and wise perspective. Remember, the components of C4 are calling, character, capability, and commissioning.

- *Calling* speaks of the heart. If a person does not have a heart to help an organization, then that person's input could be biased.

- *Character* is the product of a person's worldview. If a person's worldview is substantially different from that of the organization, there will a divergence on how to interpret events. A person who worships money will not value large investments in customer service, as these investments may be viewed as excessive and counterproductive to making money.

- *Capability* refers to a person's ability to assess the value proposition. A color-blind person will not be able to provide wise counsel on matters of color.

- *Commissioning* is the external invitation and permission that each of us needs to allow us to speak into a situation. People who have not been commissioned do not have confidence that they will be heard, and tend to not speak.

The challenge for any organization that wants to know the truth about its value proposition is to find the customers who have C4 to render the requisite input. Do not trust your own judgment; use wise counsel to validate your products. Motorola learned this lesson the hard way.

In 1994, Motorola had 60 percent of the analog cell phone market, which was primarily driven by corporate America. Digital technology was just being introduced. This technology was superior in that it was more efficient (compressible), more secure, and scalable. The cell phone market exploded worldwide. Customers were asking for digital technology, but amazingly, Motorola ignored them, choosing rather to believe that they knew more about the market than their customers. As a result, competitors began to make inroads. In 1997, Motorola belatedly launched its first digital offering, but the delay cost Motorola. By 1998, Motorola's market share dropped to 34 percent, which signaled the start of layoffs and restructuring.[6] Motorola's hubris in refusing to listen to its business customers, who provided C4 feedback, proved to be devastating.

DO NOT TRUST YOUR OWN JUDGMENT; USE WISE COUNSEL TO VALIDATE YOUR PRODUCTS.

Finding C4 employees is difficult, but finding C4 customers is even more difficult. In most cases, employers select their employees, which implies that the employers have a choice. However, many times organizations do not select their customers.

True C4 customers will have a heart to help the organization, have character alignment with the organization, and have a perspective that is meaningful and significant for the organization. The organization then must commission or embrace the customers' input. This implies that there exists a mechanism or process for collecting, analyzing, and interpreting such input. Most organizations make a perfunctory effort at gathering customer feedback. Sadly, this produces cynicism in customers and minimal beneficial information for the organization.

If an organization really wants to know the truth, it must be willing to pay the price. King Solomon expressed this reality:

Wounds from a friend can be trusted, but an enemy multiplies kisses.[7]

A true friend will tell the truth. Researchers, however, have discovered that 93 percent of Americans regularly and habitually lie in the workplace.[8] This reality only makes the task of gaining C4 feedback more arduous; hence, organizations must be very strategic at finding C4 feedback. Here are a few suggestions for consideration.

- The current model of most organizations is to make sales the top priority and service a lower priority. Consider elevating customer service by increasing the number of customer support personnel and provide toll-free numbers to make access to support faster and cheaper. Each time a customer calls, it is an opportunity to seek C4 feedback.

- Do not make customer service a profit center. Customer service's sole focus needs to be producing happy customers. The cost should be secondary. Organizations like EMC practice this reality.

- Use a customer loyalty program that is truly customer friendly and meaningful. Loyal customers should be a wonderful source of C4 feedback. Few organizations, however, seem to know how to extract this valuable information. Once when I bought my fourth car from a certain highly reputable dealership, I was told that if the dealer was my exclusive service provider that, upon trade-in, I would receive additional value for the car. Not surprisingly, this proved to be false. This loyalty program was both bogus and onerous for already loyal customers. Sadly, the dealership never sought my perspective on its loyalty program.

- Use smart systems to track customer buying trends and then shape product offerings to these trends. Seek to establish personal relationships with customers and reward them with gifts they value for providing C4 feedback. Organizations like the Beverly Hills Hotel adopt a very strategic customer preference tracking system.

In addition to making the hotel experience very easy, pleasant, and personal, the hotel offers free short-term storage to customers between visits.[9]

These are just a few examples of how to acquire C4 customer input. Yes, it is difficult and may be costly, but it is essential that every organization know the truth about its value proposition. The truth can only be discerned by gathering, analyzing, and properly interpreting C4 customer feedback. Excellent organizations will go to great lengths to discover the truth.

The Fruit of Listening to Customers: A Good Name

When senior leaders possess the Level 5 characteristics of humility and tenacity, they embrace C4 input from customers knowing that they will receive a treasure chest of input. In particular, they will glean two very important facts: the organization's reputation and what God is paying the organization to do.

A company's reputation is a key indicator of the future prospects of the organization. It is so important that King Solomon rated it above riches:

A good name is more desirable than great riches; to be esteemed is better than silver or gold.[10]

A "good name" means that customers are more than satisfied with the value proposition of the organization. The customers are so satisfied that they become unpaid public relations people—the best advertising for any organization.

REPUTATION IS PERHAPS THE MOST SUCCINCT MEASUREMENT OF THE STATE OF ANY ORGANIZATION.

Reputation is perhaps the most succinct measurement of the state of any organization. It reveals the organization's ability to compete, the quality of its service, the effectiveness of its sales effort, the efficiency of its delivery system, and the worldview encapsulated by its culture. There is no metric as pregnant with significance for an organization as its reputation.

To be efficient, organizations must know what God is funding. Level 5 leaders will discover what God is paying the organization to do. If God owns everything and is sovereignly in control, we are but stewards on earth to fulfill His pleasure. Therefore, when God desires to do something, there will be provision. Consider the following verses of Scripture:

> *I have no need of a bull from your stall or of goats from your pens, for every animal of the forest is mine, and the cattle on a thousand hills. I know every bird in the mountains, and the creatures of the field are mine.*[11]

> *Remember the former things, those of long ago; I am God, and there is no other; I am God, and there is none like me. I make known the end from the beginning, from ancient times, what is still to come. I say: My purpose will stand, and I will do all that I please. From the east I summon a bird of prey; from a far-off land, a man to fulfill my purpose. What I have said, that will I bring about; what I have planned, that will I do.*[12]

Notwithstanding that God at times allows the wicked to prosper short term, over the long term He funds that which He wishes to accomplish. Therefore, the role of senior leaders is to continually discern what God is paying for the organization to do. Sadly, most senior leaders do not seem to be doing a good job of this. According to researchers, between 90 percent and 99 percent of all new businesses started by mature companies fail.[13] This reality suggests that the senior leaders are not discerning God's will for their organizations.

Conclusion

All truly excellent organizations recognize the critical importance of customer C4 feedback to validate their value proposition and to help identify appropriate changes. Stanley Marcus, of Neiman Marcus fame, personally waited on customers from time to time, so that he could maintain the pulse of his customers. Sewell automobile dealerships place a follow-up call to every customer after either a vehicle purchase or a service visit. These calls are designed to solicit feedback from the customer and to insure customer satisfaction. Executives with Southwest Airlines hang out with customers whenever possible to hear what customers are saying.

Every great organization knows that the only way to validate its value proposition is by knowing the truth. We must all fight the temptation to self-validate and be willing to find the C4 customers who can and will speak truth to us. Only then will an organization be able to honestly validate its value proposition.

Points to Ponder

1. Describe your experience working with an organization or person who failed to solicit customer feedback.

2. Does your organization have a credible way to identify C4 customers? If so, give a brief description. If not, why not?

3. Describe your organization's customer feedback system. In what way is the feedback compromised or biased?

4. If your organization has a credible customer feedback system, is the information properly analyzed? Are the conclusions and corresponding actions helping the organization to improve?

Notes

1. Matthew 7:4–5.

2. Finkelstein, *Why Smart Executives Fail*, 56.

3. Genesis 1:28.

4. Finkelstein, *Why Smart Executives Fail*, 213–237.

5. Proverbs 28:26.

6. Finkelstein, *Why Smart Executives Fail*, 63–68.

7. Proverbs 27:6.

8. Brian Cairns, "Here's a Radical Idea—Tell the Truth!" *FastCompany*, August/September 1997, issue 10.

9. Misha Gravenor, "No Room for Mediocrity," *FastCompany*, September 2001, 160.

10. Proverbs 22:1.

11. Psalms 50:9–11.

12. Isaiah 46:9–11.

13. Andrew Campbell and Robert Park, "Stop Kissing Frogs," *HBR*, July/August 2004, 27.

Beyond Babel Model

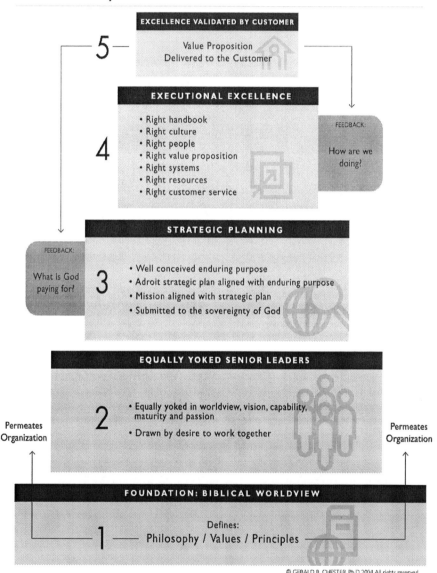

EXCELLENCE VALIDATED BY CUSTOMER

5 — Value Proposition
Delivered to the Customer

EXECUTIONAL EXCELLENCE

4
- Right handbook
- Right culture
- Right people
- Right value proposition
- Right systems
- Right resources
- Right customer service

FEEDBACK:

How are we
doing?

STRATEGIC PLANNING

FEEDBACK:

What is God
paying for?

3
- Well conceived enduring purpose
- Adroit strategic plan aligned with enduring purpose
- Mission aligned with strategic plan
- Submitted to the sovereignty of God

EQUALLY YOKED SENIOR LEADERS

2
- Equally yoked in worldview, vision, capability, maturity and passion
- Drawn by desire to work together

Permeates
Organization

Permeates
Organization

FOUNDATION: BIBLICAL WORLDVIEW

1
Defines:
Philosophy / Values / Principles

PART THREE

The Beyond Babel Model in Practice

Whatever you do, work at it with all your heart,
as working for the Lord, not for men.

If you agree with my presupposition that God has revealed, in both general and special revelation, the way that He wishes for organizations to operate, I trust that you are willing to consider the Beyond Babel Model as an approach to alignment with God. The foundation of the model is a biblical worldview, which defines a philosophy that is aligned with God. From this philosophy flow the values and principles aligned with God that will facilitate building organizations to fulfill God's mandate to man to rule His physical world. The culture of any organization is defined and expressed by the organization's philosophy, values, and principles. Only by building organizations aligned with God's philosophy, values, and principles can one build enduring world-class organizations.

The rest of the book is devoted to understanding the application of the Beyond Babel Model and comparing the model to empirical research. I trust that you will see both the power and efficacy of the Beyond Babel Model, and that you will apply yourself with all your heart to building great organizations.

Notes
Epigraph. Colossians 3:23.

Beyond Babel Model

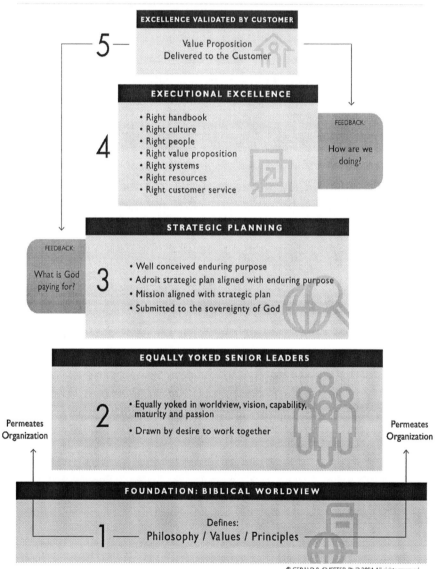

EXCELLENCE VALIDATED BY CUSTOMER

5 — Value Proposition
Delivered to the Customer

EXECUTIONAL EXCELLENCE

4
- Right handbook
- Right culture
- Right people
- Right value proposition
- Right systems
- Right resources
- Right customer service

FEEDBACK:
How are we doing?

STRATEGIC PLANNING

FEEDBACK:
What is God paying for?

3
- Well conceived enduring purpose
- Adroit strategic plan aligned with enduring purpose
- Mission aligned with strategic plan
- Submitted to the sovereignty of God

EQUALLY YOKED SENIOR LEADERS

2
- Equally yoked in worldview, vision, capability, maturity and passion
- Drawn by desire to work together

Permeates
Organization

Permeates
Organization

FOUNDATION: BIBLICAL WORLDVIEW

Defines:
1 —— Philosophy / Values / Principles

Does the Beyond Babel Model Really Work?

The typical response to the Beyond Babel Model is shock and a sense of being overwhelmed. The standard for organizational excellence seems daunting. Could any organization ever master compliance with the model? The answer is no, not completely, but that should not keep us from pursuing compliance. The mandate from God given to man in Genesis 1:26–28 challenges us, individually and organizationally, to rule by multiplying and subduing God's creation.

In what is commonly known as the Lord's prayer, alignment with God's will on earth as in heaven is a primary component.[1] The enormity and complexity of the universe suggests that the process of ruling (multiplying and subduing) is never ending. Therefore, we should not lose heart at the pursuit of mastering the universe and should realize that the work will be much more effective and productive through organizations that seek to function with excellence based on alignment with God.

Despite the obvious challenges of adopting a biblical model of organizational excellence, there are organizations that have embraced and do embrace it with success. The following case studies provide some examples to illustrate that the Beyond Babel Model really does work. Each case study illustrates compliance with the components of the Beyond Babel Model to varying degrees.

Food Store

A story has been told of a family on vacation who stopped at a fruit stand to buy some snacks.[2] The wife and daughter got out and went in. The husband and his son waited impatiently in the car. After a few minutes, which seemed interminable, the father and son went in as well. The mildly irritated father was distracted from his mission of chastisement when he noticed the cleanliness of the fruit stand. Then he noticed the excellent quality and selection of the fruit. There were no blemishes on the fruit and there was a wide selection. Digging down to the bottom of a fruit bin, he found that the quality was excellent all the way to the bottom. Then he noticed the prices were very reasonable and he observed the shopkeeper who was neatly dressed and very pleasant. His soft smile and peaceful countenance was infectious. The father thought to himself, *I have never been in a fruit stand like this before.*

The father quickly joined the other shoppers in the store, all of whom were mesmerized by the quality of the environment—the look, smell, and feel of the fruit stand was simply irresistible. The father began perusing the options to make his selections. Going to check out, he noticed again the intoxicating spirit of the shopkeeper. Kindness and love exuded from him.

As the father was walking out, he could not help but compliment the shopkeeper. Turning to him, the father said that he had never been in a fruit stand like this before. The shopkeeper smiled and said, "Thank you, but it really isn't my fruit stand." The father said, "Really? Who is the owner?" Mildly amused, the shopkeeper stated that the Lord was the owner and that he was simply the Lord's steward. And since this was the Lord's fruit stand, the shopkeeper, out of gratitude for what the Lord had done for him, wished to take very good care of His fruit stand. Furthermore, the Lord's instruction to the shopkeeper was to treat everyone the way that the shopkeeper wished to be treated.

The shopkeeper built his business around a biblical worldview. He was determined to work strategically and excellently, offering customers outstanding value. The customers could not resist the value proposition, because to the shopkeeper the bottom line was not money but obedience to the Lord.

Service Company

A friend of mine, Doug Russell, shared this story with me.[3] In the early 1990s, Doug bought a financially distressed waste collection company. Doug was a seasoned businessman with experience selling equipment to the waste collection industry. He was a Christian who believed in an integrated life, so he wanted any business that he was involved with to reflect a biblical worldview. He explained to the seller that he would be making some major changes in the business. In particular, Doug clearly communicated to the workers that he intended to follow biblical principles and practices.

Upon taking over, Doug wasted no time letting the workers know his convictions. He explained his worldview and its implications to all the workers and invited anyone who didn't agree to leave without prejudice. Several of the workers chose to leave.

Doug believed that working overtime was counterproductive. Not only were the men tired after a forty-hour week, but they needed time to be with their families, attend church, and participate in community activities. Initially, the workers were concerned because they routinely worked overtime and were accustomed to the extra income. Doug responded to their concern by raising everyone's wages to make up the difference. Also, Doug began to teach biblical principles to the workers.

Executionally, the company's service level increased. With time, the company began to gain new business as customers experienced the difference in service between Doug's company and his competitor. Finally, his competitor decided to leave the market and offered to sell his business to Doug.

Despite Doug's success with his workers and the growth of the company, the business was still not profitable. He not only paid to buy a failing company but continued to fund the negative cash flow while transforming the company into a biblically based organization. When assessing the possibility of acquiring his major competitor, he didn't see how to do it and make a profit. Explaining his assessment to his workers, they asked for a few days to assess it themselves. Doug granted their request.

By the time this opportunity came, the workers were incredibly grateful to Doug. He had demonstrated in actions that he valued them and helped them improve their lives. For workers to be treated this way is not common. So when the opportunity to help Doug came, they eagerly embraced it without Doug even asking. With deep appreciation in their hearts, the workers came to Doug and offered to take on the business from the competitor without any additional equipment or overtime. Doug reiterated that there would be no overtime. They agreed. Very shortly after the acquisition occurred, the company began to turn a profit.

Doug's commitment to a biblical model of organizational excellence finally paid off. He bought a failing business, turned the workers into happy, content, and productive workers, acquired his major competitor, and turned a failing business around.

Manufacturing Company

In 1972, Pittron Steel's unionized workers went on strike. Management by intimidation and confrontation was the philosophy of the senior leaders. This created acrimony between management and labor. Not surprisingly, sales were declining and profit was waning. Against this backdrop, Wayne Alderson was named vice president of operations. Realizing that the current approach was not working, Alderson wanted to try a different approach. As a Christian, Alderson wanted to apply biblical principles to the management of the company. With the consent of senior management, Alderson formulated Operation Turnaround. *Business Reform Magazine* carried the story in a recent article.[4]

Operation Turnaround was built on four actions, all of which were unheard of at Pittron. First, Alderson personally associated with workers and asked for their input. Second, he gave the union president an office. Third, Alderson personally greeted people at the gate at the end of each day. And fourth, Alderson shared company gasoline reserves with the workers during gas rationing days. All of these actions communicated that Alderson valued the people, wanted their perspective, and was willing to personally help them. In addition, Alderson started a regular Bible study for anyone in the company that wished to attend. All of these actions were met with incredulity. But slowly, the workers began to believe that Alderson really did value them.

The result of Operation Turnaround was stunning. Morale soared as smiles replaced frowns. Productivity rose 64 percent, sales rose 400 percent, and profit rose 30 percent. Grievances declined from twelve per week to one per year. Absenteeism declined, and quality exceeded all prior standards.

Alderson brought a biblical worldview to Pittron. He developed an equally yoked management team. His strategic plan was to build an organization that could compete with anyone in the commodity world of steel production. Executionally, Alderson used Operation Turnaround to change the culture and improve productivity. The customers validated the value proposition by increased orders leading to a dramatic increase in sales and profits.

Retail Company

An article written for *Business Reform Magazine* tells the story of the effect of applying a biblical model of excellence to a retail operation.[5] Dave Browne joined Lenscrafters in 1986 and became CEO in 1989. In the early '90s, the company was externally successful, but internally it lacked clear vision. Consequently, morale was low. Even though Lenscrafters was the market behemoth, Dave knew that the company would fail if something didn't change.

At that time Dave was a dualistic Christian; hence, he didn't understand that the Bible should provide the philosophy, values, and principles that he needed to adroitly operate Lenscrafters. He tried to practice his faith personally but his self-described management style was by "MBA standards." This meant hard driving by the numbers, aloofness, holding everyone accountable, and leaving a trail of bodies. Though the company was growing and profitable, Dave was miserable and made those around him miserable.

On a weekend retreat, Dave had an encounter with God in which he received a new perspective. Lenscrafters was not about glasses, it was about giving the gift of sight. Furthermore, God wanted Dave to run the business based on biblical principles and values.

Dave began the transformation from dualism to integration of biblical principles and values with his work. The old mission of the company was: "We exist to do business." The new mission was: "We exist to create exceptional value in the lives of customers, associates, and stakeholders."

The principle that Dave began to teach and integrate into the company was servant leadership and the key value was love. The driving questions became: Are we doing this in a way that honors God? and Are we doing this based on biblical principles and values?

THE DRIVING QUESTIONS BECAME: ARE WE DOING THIS IN A WAY THAT HONORS GOD? AND ARE WE DOING THIS BASED ON BIBLICAL PRINCIPLES AND VALUES?

Dave knew he was taking a big risk. To suddenly inject a biblical worldview into the company was very challenging. But if he was going to fail, it would be based on practicing his faith, not following the ways of the world. He knew that he had put up an invisible wall of dualism between his faith and his work that had to come down.

If a biblical worldview was going to be the basis of the company, he had to have buy-in from his senior leaders. Therefore, he set up an off-site planning meeting to share this new model of integrating biblical principles and values into the company. After confessing his own sin, he allowed discussion and built consensus for a new company vision, mission, and values.

The old strategic plan was about obtaining and maintaining the position as the largest retailer of glasses and eye exams. Success was measured in numbers of stores and profit. The new strategic plan was about sight as a gift from God. The company focused on helping the world to see and creating exceptional value for all stakeholders—customers, associates, and shareholders. Success was then defined based on serving the shareholders.

Executional excellence was achieved through operational clarity, which meant that expectations and goals were clearly defined. Tools were provided to facilitate meeting the expectations and goals. Responsibility and accountability were congruent. Workers were encouraged to go the extra mile. As much as possible, personalization was encouraged, which empowered workers to take responsibility and ownership for the delivery of the value proposition.

Best practices were the minimum acceptable performance levels. Workers were rewarded based on merit as bonuses were tied to what people could influence. The culture of the company encouraged the celebration of successes. Making work enjoyable was important because people did not need to take pain and misery home with them. They needed an enjoyable, satisfying work experience. Also, support of the community by giving back was an important value of the company.

The company embraced customer validation through customer satisfaction surveys in every store. Hearing from the customers was vital and the bonus system was tied to customer satisfaction.

Did this work? Yes, resoundingly well! Dave Browne courageously took a public company and re-engineered it based on a biblical model of excellence. Starting with a biblical worldview, he took the time to be sure that he had an equally yoked management team and a well-conceived strategic plan. Then he executed by creating a culture that valued and supported the workers. Customers validated the value proposition in every store, which enabled the company to enjoy continued success.

Financial Services

Chuck Ripka along with Duane Kropuenske raised $5.5 million from fifty investors to open a community bank in a suburb of Minneapolis. Chuck and Duane were longtime business associates who desired to work together based on Christian values. Duane knew the banking business. Chuck was a spiritually minded man who viewed himself as a pastor in business. Prior to starting the bank, Chuck had encouraged Duane's spiritual growth. Now the men wanted to integrate their Christianity into the financial services business.[6]

Starting with a dream and vision, the bank opened in March of 2003. By December 2003, its thirty workers, all of whom were Christians, built an impressive loan portfolio based on deposits of $43 million, more than three times the planned $14 million. In addition, because of the bank's holistic approach that ministers to both physical and spiritual needs, forty-seven customers accepted Jesus Christ as Savior and numerous customers experienced physical healings.

Customers walk into the bank and note a cornerstone that reads "In God We Trust." Once inside, the artwork testifies to the faith of the senior leaders of the bank. Customers comment about the peace they feel in the bank. On one occasion a person came into the bank and said that she didn't know why she was there. Something was drawing her. The employee to whom the person was speaking commented about the Christian perspective embraced by the bank management. The person immediately stated that she was a Christian, to which the employee noted that the common faith was clearly the draw.

The culture of the bank encourages workers to pray and counsel with the customers about financial and spiritual matters. Prayer for various needs is a frequent occurrence. Customers can ask for prayer and if bank workers sense a need they can volunteer to pray. Even customers in the drive-through line can receive prayer from the teller. This personal ministry does not interfere with the operation of the bank. In fact, the personal ministry flows smoothly with the environment, since the culture embraces everyone holistically. That is, spiritual and physical matters are both valued and considered during each transaction and customer interaction.

Unlike most banks, the loan officers make loans based on both the numbers and their hearts. For example, a couple applied for a loan to refinance their home. The husband, who was self-employed, had experienced a business failure. While he was seeking employment, the couple got behind on their house payments. Finally, the husband was able to secure a good job, but by then the couple was seriously delinquent with numerous creditors, including the mortgage company. Despite the husband's new job, the mortgage company chose to foreclose rather than to give the couple time to catch up on their payments. The couple came to Chuck for help.

Chuck prayerfully considered the matter. He realized the couple had experienced some difficult times and made some poor choices. But the husband and wife were people of good character and appeared to learn from their mistakes. Chuck realized that the couple's poor credit rating was an aberration and did not really reflect their willingness and ability to pay their obligations. He also noted that the loan-to-value ratio of 60 percent was favorable. Relying on his spiritual senses, the loan-to-value ratio, and the character of the people, he overlooked the bad credit rating and made the loan. This was a decision that few bankers would have made, but it reflected the reality of the situation and the compassion of the bank. As a result, the couple enjoyed keeping their home with a reduction in monthly payments. The bank has a grateful new customer and a new performing loan.

> THE BIBLICALLY BASED CULTURE OF THE BUSINESS ENCOURAGES HOLISTIC TREATMENT OF PEOPLE.

The bank is led by two men who are equally yoked and rooted in a biblical worldview. Their strategic plan is to build a community financial services business that is integrated holistically with their Christian faith. The biblically based culture of the business encourages holistic treatment of people. Both spiritual needs and physical needs are treated as important. Customers validated the value proposition by depositing $43 million in the bank during the first ten months of operation.

Medical Service Company

J. Victor Eagan is a dentist who operates an orthodontics practice in Detroit. Dr. Eagan's story was carried in *Charisma* magazine.[7] He is a Christian who embraces a biblical worldview and seeks to integrate it into every area of his life, including his business. He looks to the Bible to define principles and values of the practice and seeks to stay dependent on the Holy Spirit for guidance. Every employee seeks to integrate his or her Christian faith at work, so Dr. Eagan enjoys an equally yoked team. His strategic plan is to advance the kingdom of God in the practice by touching his patients with loving holistic dental service. Executionally, his workers have regular meetings for prayer and Bible study. The screen savers on the computers have a Christian theme. Every employee is encouraged to pray for the patients. Patients are encouraged to share prayer requests. A team of intercessors faithfully prays for each patient and employee. The waiting room is stocked with Christian videos and literature. From time to time, Dr. Eagan provides pro bono services.

The validation of Dr. Eagan's value proposition can be seen anecdotally in a story about a Jewish patient. Despite the overt and obvious Christian theme, a Jewish man kept coming to Dr. Eagan because he "felt the presence of the Lord there." In the fall of 2002, the Jewish man was killed in a work-related accident. The next day, the man's widow kept her children's appointments with Dr. Eagan because as she said, "I knew you would treat me nicely and love me." A week later, she came back to the office and said that coming to Dr. Eagan's office the day after her husband died was the only thing that stabilized her and enabled her to retain her sanity.

Dr. Eagan and his staff deliver excellent dental care. The practice is rooted in a biblical worldview. The staff is an equally yoked team executing a well-conceived strategic plan with a value proposition that is so compelling that even non-Christians value it.

Public Policy

In 1824, the Glasglow Missionary Society established the Lovedale mission station in the cape province of South Africa. The local community was rife with slave trading, tribal warfare, and primitive barbarism. Nevertheless, the Scottish Presbyterians sought to evangelize the local community for over forty years. They saw little fruit. In 1867, the missionary society decided to cut its losses and abandon the station.

Around the same time, a young man by the name of James Stewart arrived in South Africa with a vision to help develop commercial enterprises in Africa. Quickly, he realized that the people did not have enough basic life and work skills to be able to function in commercial organizations. So he proposed to turn the Lovedale mission station into a school to educate and train the indigenous population. The Glasglow Missionary Society granted him the use of the facility.

For the next thirty-eight years, Stewart taught the people biblical worldview and life skills. The people began to build commercial organizations to farm the land, build roads and buildings, process food, print literature, make wagons, care for horses, and so forth. The chaotic pagan society was transformed into a productive God-honoring community that impacted all of South Africa. Stewart was so successful at transforming the society that Nelson Mandela called him a "model Christian."

The forty-year effort to evangelize by the Glasglow Missionary Society was virtually fruitless. But the next forty years of teaching and training a biblical worldview, including life skills, to a pagan people transformed the community and impacted a country. Stewart demonstrated that integrated Christianity works. When evangelism is made the goal, there is little fruit.

But if the goal is to teach and train a biblical worldview in all of life, the result is transformation of people.

WHEN EVANGELISM IS MADE THE GOAL, THERE IS LITTLE FRUIT.

Stewart used a biblical model of organizational excellence. Beginning with a biblical worldview, he built an equally yoked team. His strategic plan was rooted in the reality that a biblical education and perspective were necessary to facilitate commercial activity. For thirty-eight years, he taught local people a biblical worldview and trained them in practical commercial skills. The value proposition was so powerful that the whole country was touched by the transformed society in the heart of South Africa.[8]

Conclusion

Does the Beyond Babel Model of organizational excellence work? I contend that it does. Not only does the model find its basis in biblical truth, but pragmatically it works. This chapter presented anecdotal evidence of this fact by looking at numerous case studies. Each case study illustrated the benefits of applying a biblical worldview to the organization. In each case, the result was powerful transformation of the organization. All stakeholders were winners. Excellent products and services were delivered. Financial blessing was the fruit. Political and social blessings came from following a biblical worldview. Customers validated the value propositions as witnessed by the growth and prosperity of the organizations.

The reality is clear and compelling. If the God of the Bible made the universe, surely He made the rules for all the games that man must play—personal, family, church, work, and government. Therefore, organizational excellence and prosperity are rooted in alignment with a biblical worldview. Building on this, equally yoked senior leaders adroitly develop strategic plans that are executed with excellence by people empowered by the culture and resources of the organization to deliver a well-conceived value proposition. Customers validate the value proposition with feedback that allows the organization to make appropriate corrections to its value proposition. The result is an enduring, excellent, and prosperous organization.

Points to Ponder

1. Compare the following organizations in your life to the Beyond Babel Model. Specifically, assess each organization against the five key elements of the model (biblical worldview, equally yoked senior leadership, strategic planning, executional excellence, and customer feedback):

    Family

    Church

    Business

    Community Government

2. In your experience, have you seen an organization that uses the Beyond Babel Model? If so, describe the organization and its value proposition.

Notes

1. Matthew 6:10.

2. Source unknown.

3. Private communication.

4. Rick Williams, "People at the Top Equals Profit at the Bottom," *Business Reform Magazine*, vol. 3, no. 1, January/February 2003, 28–29.

5. "The Holy See," *Business Reform Magazine*, vol. 3, no. 1, January/February 2003, 20–23.

6. Private communication.

7. "God@Work," *Charisma*, June 2003.

8. George Grant, "The Adullam Strategy," *Tabletalk*, January 2003, 59–60.

Beyond Babel Model

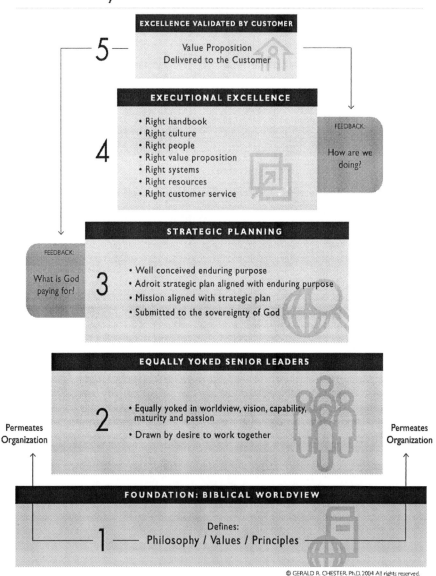

EXCELLENCE VALIDATED BY CUSTOMER

5 — Value Proposition
Delivered to the Customer

EXECUTIONAL EXCELLENCE

4
- Right handbook
- Right culture
- Right people
- Right value proposition
- Right systems
- Right resources
- Right customer service

FEEDBACK:
How are we doing?

STRATEGIC PLANNING

FEEDBACK:
What is God paying for?

3
- Well conceived enduring purpose
- Adroit strategic plan aligned with enduring purpose
- Mission aligned with strategic plan
- Submitted to the sovereignty of God

EQUALLY YOKED SENIOR LEADERS

2
- Equally yoked in worldview, vision, capability, maturity and passion
- Drawn by desire to work together

Permeates Organization

Permeates Organization

FOUNDATION: BIBLICAL WORLDVIEW

1
Defines:
Philosophy / Values / Principles

Is the Beyond Babel Model Consistent with Empirical Research?

Numerous researchers have sought to understand the characteristics of excellent organizations. Generally, researchers approach the study pragmatically with little consideration to the worldview of the organizations studied. In other words, researchers are not looking for ideology but merely seeking to discover the operating practices that work.

This chapter compares three empirical studies to the Beyond Babel Model. My thesis is that the degree of enduring excellence enjoyed by an organization depends on the degree to which that organization aligns itself, either wittingly or unwittingly, with God's principles. This is a logical corollary of the axiomatic truth that God created the universe and made the rules for all the games. Hence, one would expect that there are no principles, except God's principles, that will facilitate enduring success. Furthermore, the principles discovered by honest and accurate pragmatic research can only be God's principles.

Since the biblical worldview that undergirds this book assumes that the God of the Bible created the universe, one would expect that pragmatic empirical studies of organizational performance would be consistent with the Beyond Babel Model. I contend that the various studies are consistent with the Beyond Babel Model and further assert that the model is comprehensive in that the results of the empirical studies are all contained in the Beyond Babel Model. To support this thesis, consider the Evergreen Project and the books *Good to Great* and *Discovering the Soul of Service.* See Appendix II for more comparisons.

> **THE DEGREE OF ENDURING EXCELLENCE ENJOYED BY AN ORGANIZATION DEPENDS ON THE DEGREE TO WHICH THAT ORGANIZATION ALIGNS ITSELF WITH GOD'S PRINCIPLES.**

The Evergreen Project

A great example of research rooted in pragmatism is the Evergreen Project.[1] This project uncovered two categories of characteristics, primary and secondary, that facilitate organizational excellence. The study defines success primarily financially. In a biblical worldview, financial measures are one gauge of success but not *the* gauge.

This project studied over two hundred different well-established management practices, seeking to understand what really works. Much to the dismay of the researchers, they discovered that most of the management tools and techniques studied did not directly contribute to superior organizational performance. They concluded that the key to excellent organizational performance is found in four basic management practices: strategy, execution, culture, and structure. Coupled with these basic practices, excellent organizations practice two of four secondary management practices: talent, innovation, leadership, and mergers and acquisitions (M&A).

All four basic or primary management practices are contained in the Beyond Babel Model. *Strategy* and *execution* are, respectively, the third and fourth building blocks of the model. *Culture* refers to the environment of an organization that is defined by its philosophy, values, and principles. *Structure* is another element of executional excellence. Structure refers to the need for simple efficacious operating practices. Unnecessary bureaucracy and antiquated practices are eliminated by organizations that achieve excellent performance.

The Evergreen Project Compared to the **Beyond Babel Model**							
Primary Management Practices (Winners have 4 of 4)				**Secondary Management Practices** (Winners have 2 of 4)			
STRATEGY	EXECUTION	CULTURE	STRUCTURE	TALENT	INNOVATION	LEADERSHIP	M&A
Validation							
Execution	○		○	○	○		○
Strategic Plan ○							
Unified Leaders				○		○	
Worldview		○					

Diagram 6

The secondary management practices—talent, innovation, leadership, and M&A—are also included in the Beyond Babel Model. Using the C4 principle as the criteria for hiring people insures that the organization has the right talent. Innovation is the product of an organization that embraces the biblical mandate to subdue the earth.[2] Leadership is covered by equally yoked senior leaders. M&A is part of strategic planning and fulfilled in executional excellence.

The primary and secondary components of the Evergreen Project are included in the Beyond Babel Model. Diagram 6 shows the relationships between the Beyond Babel Model and the empirical characteristics of the Evergreen Project.

Good to Great

Business guru Jim Collins spent 10.5 people-years and $1 million seeking to understand the characteristics that enable good companies to become great companies. In his book, *Good to Great*,[3] he studied eleven public companies. Each company was compared to another well-respected or good company in the same industry. The question was: What made the great companies perform in a superior manner to the good companies as measured by stock price performance over fifteen years? Collins extracted seven key principles from his research. Each of these principles, as noted in Diagram 7, fits into the Beyond Babel Model.

Good to Great Model Compared to the **Beyond Babel Model**

	LEVEL 5 LEADERS	THE RIGHT PEOPLE	STOCKDALE PARADOX	HEDGEHOG CONCEPT	CULTURE OF DISCIPLINE	TECHNOLOGY ACCELERATORS	FLY WHEEL DOOM LOOP
Validation							
Execution		O			O	O	O
Strategic Plan			O				
Unified Leaders	O						
Worldview				O			

Diagram 7

1. Level 5 Leaders

These leaders are characterized by unremitting tenacity combined with personal humility and selflessness. Personal agendas are subordinated to the good of the organization. Level 5 leaders build multigenerational organizations that do not depend on them. Such organizations exist to accomplish the mission of the organization rather than stroking the personal ego of the leaders. In the Beyond Babel Model, Level 5 leaders are part of the second building block— unified, equally yoked senior leaders. Each senior leader needs to display Level 5 characteristics of humility and tenacity if the organization is to enjoy the foundation that will facilitate excellence.

2. First Who ... Then What

To accomplish a mission, an organization must function as a team. Like a football team going to the Super Bowl, the organization must have the right people. Having the right people encompasses many characteristics. Clearly there must be the right blend of skills plus alignment with the organization's philosophy, values, and principles. This is a predicate of the fourth building block of the Beyond Babel Model—executional excellence.

3. Stockdale Paradox

Named after the highest-ranking POW in the Vietnam War prison camp known as the Hanoi Hilton, this principle simply states that one must face the brutal facts but never lose faith. A key element of a biblical worldview is faith: faith that the world is much more complex than any one human or group of humans can hope to master or control. Therefore, to succeed individually and organizationally, one must never deny reality. Dealing in truth is the only way to move forward and solve problems. No matter how difficult the truth may be, one must always believe that somehow, someway he or she will prevail. Truth is a basic principle of a biblical worldview.

4. Hedgehog Concept

This principle illustrates the power of simplicity and focus. The simple, singular defense mechanism of the hedgehog is used as a metaphor to demonstrate the efficacy of simplicity. To be excellent, organizations must have a clear focus. No organization can be all things to all people. Most organizations can only do one thing really well; hence, to be excellent, organizations must be laser focused. Furthermore, the focus needs to be uncomplicated. Great organizations work to find the bulls-eye for their value proposition.

Collins uses three intersecting circles to illustrate how to find the organization's bulls-eye. The three circles represent the organization's passion, skill, and key financial driver. The intersection of all three circles defines the bulls-eye, which provides the singular focus for the organization. In the Beyond Babel Model, the "hedgehog concept" is a key element of strategic planning. Strategic planning is about clarifying what an organization is to do and how it is to do it.

5. Culture of Discipline

To execute well requires discipline. Management teams need discipline to define a strategic plan and stay the course. There needs to be a culture of discipline to execute the plan well. A by-product of discipline is accountability. No organization can achieve and sustain world-class excellence without accountability. In the Beyond Babel Model, discipline is a critical element of executional excellence.

6. Technology Accelerators

Collins asserts that technology is not a major driver of organizational excellence; rather it is an accelerator or an enhancer. In the Beyond Babel Model, technology is a tool that enhances all aspects of the organization, particularly the execution.

7. Fly Wheel and Doom Loop

The fly wheel is the principle of building by first crawling, then walking, and finally running. Starting from a dead stop and moving to a full run rapidly is challenging for anyone. Sustained growing excellence is built on the fly wheel principle of ever-increasing momentum. As a fly wheel begins to turn faster and faster, the growing momentum makes it very difficult to stop. To successfully stop a fly wheel requires much effort.

On the other hand, the doom loop is the result of failing to build a proper foundation to support organizational growth. Trying to go from a dead stop to a full run is rife with challenges and, frequently, ends in failure. In the Beyond Babel Model, the fly wheel principle is endemic throughout. From developing an organizational philosophy on a biblical worldview, to building the equally yoked management team, to developing an effective strategic plan, to executing the plan with excellence, to gathering and properly interpreting customer feedback, every step of the Beyond Babel Model requires adherence to the fly wheel principle.

The principles uncovered by Collins are all contained in the Beyond Babel Model. This is because Collins simply uncovered the reality that the God of the Bible, who created the universe, also created the principles that facilitate organizational excellence.

Discovering the Soul of Service

Like other research projects, Leonard Berry investigated a set of carefully chosen organizations to determine the keys to sustainable success

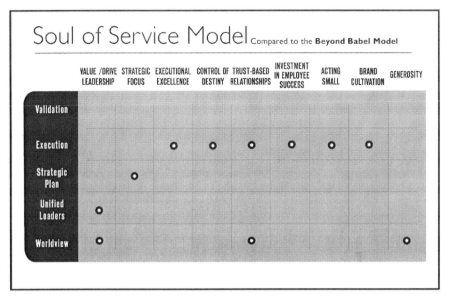

Diagram 8

in the service business.[4] Unlike *Built to Last* (see Appendix II) and *Good to Great* that focused on publicly held companies, Berry's sample set included both publicly and privately held service organizations. Furthermore, he purposefully examined both small and large organizations. The sample set of fourteen organizations was selected based on both sustained customer acceptance and financial success. As with the other studies, a set of principles was posited as the reason that the organizations were able to sustain excellent service.

The following discussion shows that Berry's proposed principles are contained within the Beyond Babel Model (see Diagram 8).

1. Value Driven Leadership

This study recognizes the importance of character-based leadership. Berry proposes seven core values that each of the organizations in the study embraces. These values are excellence, innovation, joy, teamwork, respect, integrity, and social profit. The fact that each of the fourteen organizations embraces these values suggests that the core values are not arbitrary. This is not surprising. If one believes in divine design, one would expect that there is a set of universal core values that will facilitate sustained excellent service. As obvious as this may be, the reality is difficult for a society steeped in humanistic thinking to perceive.

Clearly such a proposition is very consistent with the Beyond Babel Model. Unified senior leaders who embrace a biblical worldview find that biblical values provide the foundation of excellent organizations.

2. Strategic Focus

Sustained excellent service requires keen focus. No organization can be all things to all people. Every organization that wishes to provide sustained superior service must develop sharp focus. This focus is the product of adroit strategic planning. Strategic planning is the unrelenting iterative and heuristic process that defines the value proposition and requisite delivery mechanism of the organization with ultra-sharp clarity. Competing agendas are eliminated regardless of how financially or emotionally attractive.

This principle is the essence of the third building block of the Beyond Babel Model—strategic planning.

3. Executional Excellence

No organization can deliver sustained excellent service without unrelenting impeccable execution. To perform at this level requires extensive planning and training coupled with a culture that invites and rewards going the extra mile. Workers throughout the organization must be alert, proactive problem solvers. When executional excellence is a priority, there is no place for excuses. The only thing that counts is performance on a world-class level. This characteristic is the product of an organization with a clear strategic focus led by a management team that embraces biblical principles and values.

This characteristic is the fourth building block of the Beyond Babel Model.

4. Control of Destiny

This label is misleading in that no one really has control over his or her destiny. The universe is much too big for anyone or any organization to really control. What is meant by this principle is that excellent service organizations have a very clear, focused, unfettered mission. Any opportunity that does not contribute to the mission of the organization is a distraction and therefore eliminated from consideration.

Within the Beyond Babel Model, this principle of unfettered organizational focus is part of the fourth building block—executional excellence. Every world-class organization is keenly focused on its mission and refuses to be deterred.

5. Trust Based Relationships

Within the culture of every truly outstanding organization is a sense of mutual trust. Without trust no one feels free to take risks. Without taking risks, very little will be accomplished. If everyone is playing it safe, the organization is not moving forward, which means that it is moving backward.

Executional excellence, as defined in the Beyond Babel Model, requires a culture of trust among the workers, vendors, and customers. A culture of trust is a product of walking in a biblical worldview. Trust means that everyone is operating by the Golden Rule. The Golden Rule is about love, the highest of all values. This means that each person is supporting and assuming the best about everyone. Such a culture does not ignore the reality of sin, but it is not so jaundiced or paranoid to assume that no one is trustworthy. Individuals who prove to be untrustworthy are impediments to the organization's ability to deliver an excellent value proposition.

6. Investment in Employee Success

People who are individually successful build successful organizations. This principle embraces the reality of individual purpose and destiny. Organizational excellence is the collective by-product of the individual excellence of each member of the organization. Therefore, for any organization to be truly great, it must be built by people who know who they are, why they are on planet earth, and are committed to fulfilling their purpose by living in a biblical worldview.

This principle is a key element of executional excellence, the fourth building block of the Beyond Babel Model.

7. Acting Small

The larger the organization, the more impersonal it seems to be. This means that the quality of service usually declines with an organization's size. In order to maintain a high level of service, a large organization must adopt a cultural practice of acting and thinking like a smaller organization. Workers must think of themselves as proprietors or faithful stewards. Faithful stewards take responsibility as if they personally own whatever they have stewardship over. When this practice becomes ubiquitous throughout an organization, the service delivered becomes stellar.

In the Beyond Babel Model, the principle of faithful stewardship is rooted in a biblical worldview and is a key ingredient of executional excellence.

8. Brand Cultivation

The salient features of a value proposition are contained within an organization's brand. For any organization, there is nothing that communicates the essence of the organization more than its brand. Every great organization works hard to develop and promote its brand identity. The brand is what people remember and, many times, is a critical element in accepting the value proposition of an organization.

In the Beyond Babel Model, branding is a vital step in the fourth building block—executional excellence.

9. Generosity

Being generous is a characteristic of virtually every enduring, successful organization. It represents an attitude and perspective that acknowledge that we humans are all part of the same community. In any community, there are always needs. Sensitive caring people seek to help those in need, particularly those who can't help themselves. Great service organizations understand the importance of giving and helping the community and those in need. These organizations proactively seek to give. This perspective is part of the company culture. Practicing generosity brings blessing to the organization because of the principle of sowing and reaping. When any organization sows kindness and care, it will reap a good reward.

Clearly, this is a biblical principle and reflects a biblical worldview toward charity. A biblical worldview is the foundational building block of the Beyond Babel Model.

Discovering the Soul of Service presents the importance of a high value system perhaps better than the other studies. It unambiguously stresses the importance of equally yoked leaders who lead based on a high value system. Unwittingly, the author has embraced principles that can all easily be related to the Beyond Babel Model.

Conclusion

This chapter compares the components of excellent organizations presented by three empirical studies to the Beyond Babel Model. The measure for success or excellence used by the studies is financial. The biblical definition of excellence includes financial measures but also includes a broader definition based on righteousness as defined in the Bible. In truly excellent organizations, pragmatism is submitted to principle; righteous conduct trumps money.[5]

> **THE BEYOND BABEL MODEL IS NOT** *DEFINED* **PRAGMATICALLY, BUT IT** *IS CONFIRMED* **PRAGMATICALLY.**

The focus of the studies is primarily executional excellence, most likely because of the pragmatic nature of the target audience. Executional excellence is rooted in values and principles that each organization chooses to practice. Values and principles are rooted in the philosophy or worldview embraced by the most influential leaders of the organization. Some researchers do recognize the importance of core values and principles and even acknowledge that there is an underlying philosophy that defines the values and principles of organization. But researchers do not seem to understand the source of either the philosophy or the values and principles. Nor do they seem interested in finding the source. Such a position is unsatisfactory, particularly to those who believe that the universe was designed by an intelligent being.

The Beyond Babel Model is not *defined* pragmatically, but it is *confirmed* pragmatically. It logically follows that if the God of the Bible created the universe and reveals Himself to His creatures through the Bible, honest research will discover that the principles that facilitate organizational excellence are biblical principles. For more model comparisons, please see Appendix II.

Points to Ponder

1. Consider any organization that performs at a world-class level. What are the key principles that facilitate this performance? Can you tie these principles to the Bible?

2. Can you identify any operating principles that facilitate building excellent enduring organizations that cannot be tied to Bible? If so, list the principles.

3. Select any organization you wish (your family, business, local government, etc.). List some ways the organization could improve through the application of the Beyond Babel Model.

Notes

1. Nohria, Joyce, and Roberson, "What Really Works," *Harvard Business Review*, July 2003, 42–52.

2. Genesis 1:26–28.

3. Jim Collins, *Good to Great* (NY: Harper Business, 2001).

4. Berry, *Discovering the Soul of Service*, 1999.

5. Proverbs 22:1.

Beyond Babel Model

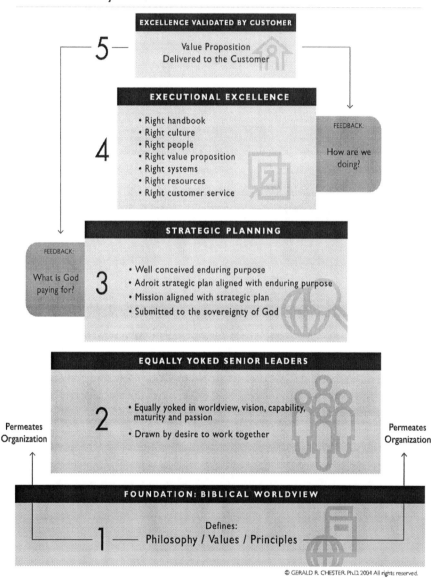

EXCELLENCE VALIDATED BY CUSTOMER

5 — Value Proposition
Delivered to the Customer

EXECUTIONAL EXCELLENCE

4
- Right handbook
- Right culture
- Right people
- Right value proposition
- Right systems
- Right resources
- Right customer service

FEEDBACK:

How are we doing?

STRATEGIC PLANNING

FEEDBACK:

What is God paying for?

3
- Well conceived enduring purpose
- Adroit strategic plan aligned with enduring purpose
- Mission aligned with strategic plan
- Submitted to the sovereignty of God

EQUALLY YOKED SENIOR LEADERS

2
- Equally yoked in worldview, vision, capability, maturity and passion
- Drawn by desire to work together

Permeates Organization

Permeates Organization

FOUNDATION: BIBLICAL WORLDVIEW

1 —— Defines:
Philosophy / Values / Principles

Why Are There So Few Excellent Organizations?

Most of us have heard the expression *caveat emptor* or "buyer beware." This phrase is a warning to buyers to carefully check out a product before buying. Among wise people, it is an operating principle that is used in virtually every significant purchase. The fact that people feel compelled to practice *caveat emptor* is a testimony to the lack of quality of the value proposition of most sellers. The goal of many sellers is simply to make the sale. There is little concern about the buyers, so they become suspicious and cynical.

The conclusion of many is that there are few excellent organizations as reflected by the reality that there are few really excellent value propositions. Instead, the majority of organizations fail, a lot are mediocre, some are good, and a very few are excellent. Why is this?

Michael Gerber asserts that 80 percent of all businesses will fail in the first five years of existence.[1] He also articulates the fatal assumption that is at the root of most business failures: "If you understand the technical work of a business, you understand a business that does technical work."[2] From my experience, I concur with both of these assertions. This means that most business startups are inherently flawed from inception, so failure is to be expected.

The Threat of Mediocrity

For many organizations mediocrity is the stage that precedes failure. It is the place where the value proposition doesn't stand. Customers buying the products or services from a mediocre organization will be dissatisfied. After all, who wants to buy mediocre products and services? Mediocrity opens the door for excellence. When excellence appears on the scene in the form of a competitor, mediocrity's days are numbered. Someone may make the mistake of buying mediocre products and services once, maybe twice, but soon the draw to excellence will undercut mediocrity and hasten its demise.

Jim Collins argues that good is the enemy of great.[3] Good leads to complacency. It is built on compromise. It makes one satisfied with a standard that is not really excellent. Organizations that move beyond mediocrity often find it difficult to move beyond good. So what's wrong with good? Good makes us settle for less than the best. It lures us into thinking that we don't need to try harder or be more creative. Who wants to be part of something good when one could be part of something really great? Who wants to buy a good value proposition when one could buy an excellent value proposition?

The Missing Foundation

So if one is convinced that being part of an excellent organization is a noble objective, how does one find such an organization? The answer is to use the Beyond Babel Model, which consists of the following key elements: alignment with a biblical worldview, equally yoked senior leaders, strategic thinking, executional excellence, and performance validation by customers.

The foundation of the Beyond Babel Model is a biblical worldview. By this I mean that the philosophy, principles, and values of the organization are defined by the Bible. The Bible is then the primary handbook for management and operational practices. To prosper under God's system means that organizations must be aligned with God.

Consider, for example, a simple principle such as honoring the Sabbath. In the account of the Creation, God blessed the Sabbath and made it a holy day.[4] R. G. LeTourneau knew this principle and was convicted when he failed to practice it, which led to a very difficult situation for him.

In 1931, R. G. was a forty-three-year-old dirt contractor who worked hard to overcome a business failure that occurred earlier in his life. He procured contracts to build roads, dams, and other projects where large quantities of the earth needed to be relocated. Because there were few machines available to assist with such arduous work in the early part of the twentieth century, he designed and built his own machines.

Despite the depression, 1930 was a very good year for R. G. Revenue was $100,000+ and profit $30,000+. (Multiply by ten to get current dollars.) The next year was looking even better. He had a contract to build a road to the site where Boulder Dam would be built and he had a contract to build an earth dam in Orange County, California. In addition, he had a new plant for building his equipment.

Despite entering 1931 with high expectations, something went terribly wrong with the Boulder Road project. The test bores missed the presence of extensive hard rock deposits that had to be penetrated to build the road. R. G.'s bid did not include any allowance for these hidden conditions. As a result, he finished the job more than $100,000 in debt, which happened to be his total revenue for the prior year.

Wounded but not dead, he forged on hoping to recover the loss on the earth dam project. As you might expect, he was under a lot of pressure from the bonding company, creditors, and the state. The bonding company and creditors were concerned about his financial condition, which was not good. In fact, the bonding company was so concerned that an on-site representative was assigned to the earth dam project. The state wanted the job completed before the fall rains. Since he was late starting the job because of the problems on the Boulder Road project, the state was rightfully concerned.

Initially, the state did not want him to start the job, but they gave him a test to see if he could work fast enough to make the schedule. The test was to build the base of the dam in one month. The base would hold very little water and pose no serious threat if the dam was not completed until later. Despite the fact that his people did not believe it could be done, they worked seven days a week and miraculously passed the test of moving 400,000 cubic yards of dirt in one month.

Passing this test was crucial for the survival of R. G.'s company, which was teetering on the precipice of bankruptcy. Clearly, everyone was thrilled that they passed the test. R. G., however, became very concerned about working his men seven days a week. He had worked them for a month without a break and was given the go-ahead to complete the project based on the demonstrated production capability. R. G. wanted to give his men a break. In fact, he wanted to give them a day off every week. The bonding company's on-site representative was not pleased. He believed that working seven days a week was necessary to complete the project on schedule. Nevertheless, R. G. gave his men the next Sunday off.

Sunday morning the only people on the job were the bonding company representative and his assistant. Given R. G.'s financial condition, the bonding company stood to take the hit if R. G. was late completing the project, so the bonding company representative was very angry. Monday morning, the bonding company representative gave R. G. a very impassioned piece of his mind and then marched off to report the situation to Mr. Hall, his boss at the home office in San Francisco. Immediately, Mr. Hall called R. G. and asked if R. G. had received the $30,000 check. (Apparently the bonding company was making the progress payments.) R. G. indicated that he had; Mr. Hall told him not to cash it and that he was coming down. It appeared that the bonding company was going to foreclose and take over the job.

The reason that R. G. was determined to give his men a day off every week was that he believed that a Sabbath[5] rest was the teaching of Scripture. R. G. was a Christian and believed that the Bible provided him with the principles by which he was to live his life, including his business life. Unlike what is happening today where God is being removed from business, R. G. was seeking to integrate the teaching of the Bible into every area of his life.

R. G. was determined to honor the Sabbath for he believed that it was what he must do to honor God. He was so convicted of this reality that he was willing to turn his company over to the bonding company, if need be. No matter what, he was going to be true to his faith. Given his convictions, the only thing that R. G. could do was pray. He didn't pray for the Lord to save his company. He prayed, rather, for the ability to honor God by observing a weekly Sabbath.

In those days, the road system in the United States was not well developed. A trip from San Francisco to Orange County, which was several hundred miles, could take more than a full day. When Mr. Hall left his office in San Francisco, he was determined to foreclose on R. G. On the way, however, something happened, something that even Mr. Hall could not explain: Mr. Hall changed his mind. When he arrived at the project site, he asked R. G. if he could complete the project on schedule working six days a week. R. G. indicated that he believed he could. Mr. Hall told R. G. to go ahead and cash the progress payment check and to take Sundays off.

R. G. was stunned. He fully expected to be terminated by the bonding company and thus be out of business. This meant he would be jobless and $100,000 in debt. Just a dozen years prior, he had gone broke in the car repair business and ended up $500 in debt. The thought of being $100,000 in debt, with no means to pay it or support his family, was a daunting thought. Deep down, he knew that God had answered his prayer. God granted him the favor he was seeking—the ability to honor God by observing the Sabbath. So R. G. and his company continued on the project, finishing it on time and within budget.

This experience didn't solve all of R. G.'s problems. He finished the job and made a small profit, but not enough to pay off the $100,000 debt. In time, however, he did pay it off, but that's another story. The lesson that R.G. learned on the earth dam project was incredible and it served him the rest of his life. He learned that following God's principles is the key to favor and prosperity. The God of the Bible made it clear that He blesses obedience and curses disobedience.[6] By simply standing on his convictions, R. G. saw God's favor at work in a remarkable way. What could R. G. do to change Mr. Hall's mind when he was determined to foreclose? The only thing R. G. could do was pray.

> **FOLLOWING GOD'S PRINCIPLES IS THE KEY TO FAVOR AND PROSPERITY.**

Knowing the risk of defying the will of the bonding company, R. G. had stood fast with his decision not to work on Sundays, for he knew that continuing to dishonor God was a greater risk. Did he want to risk the judgment of God or of the bonding company? While the judgment of men is only finite, the judgment of God has eternal implications. So regardless of the response of the bonding company, R. G. knew that he could not defy God.

The temptation to compromise is enormous for all of us. Compromise appears to have an immediate reward—it relieves pressure. But in the end it does not lead to prosperity. When the federal government compromises a balanced budget and spends more than it takes in, what happens? There is an apparent short-term benefit, but soon inflation and the burden of paying off the debt must be faced. When companies, such as Enron, choose to capitulate to the pressure of producing quarterly earnings growth, lies and deception become an acceptable compromise; but in the end, lies and deception do not bring prosperity.

COMPROMISE APPEARS TO HAVE AN IMMEDIATE REWARD—IT RELIEVES PRESSURE. BUT IN THE END IT DOES NOT LEAD TO PROSPERITY.

If God created the universe, He alone made all the rules for the games—personal, family, church, business, and government. If He made the rules, doesn't He prosper those who follow His rules? What happens to those who don't follow His rules; to those who choose to make up their own rules?

R. G. was determined to align his life and business with God's principles. And so he did, going on to become one of the most famous businessmen of the twentieth century. His autobiography is titled *R. G. LeTourneau: Mover of Men and Mountains*. He was, indeed, a mover of men and mountains. The reason for his success was simple. He was a man who, regardless of the price, learned to obey God in his business practices. As a result, God's favor shined on him brightly. He was a man who prospered, who understood that the key to prosperity was alignment with the Creator. After all, the Creator makes the rules for all the games and blesses those who align their lives with His principles.

Conclusion

The reason there is a dearth of excellent organizations is that few learn the lesson of alignment with a biblical worldview. Most organizations follow the path of least resistance, that is, popular thinking. This path leads to dualism since society seems determined to remove God from public policy, education, and business. God and spirituality are relegated to a place of secondary importance. For many, God is irrelevant. For others who wish to acknowledge

God, the easy way to do it is on Sunday when no one really cares or notices.

Even for those who resist this dualistic mentality, all too often there is little understanding of biblical reality in organizational behavior, even among churches, because biblical worldview applied to everyday work life is not widely taught beyond ethics and evangelism. It is the rare church that teaches such critical topics as organizational behavior, management, leadership, finance, human resources, and strategic thinking from a biblical worldview.

This reality explains why there are so few excellent organizations. Few people really believe that God made the rules for all the games, so His handbook for organizational behavior (the Bible) is not used to define the philosophy, values, and principles of organizational behavior. Instead, corporate America submits to the philosophies of business pundits such as Peter Drucker, Jim Collins, and Tom Peters. Unfortunately, I have yet to see in these men an understanding of a biblical worldview.

If the presuppositions about God as the Creator and the Bible as His revelation are truth, a business philosophy without a foundation in a biblical perspective must be inherently flawed. Nevertheless, it is rare to find a leader who embraces the Bible as the foundational book for business philosophy. As there are few leaders who do, it is not surprising that few organizations ever achieve excellence. Those that do achieve a level of sustained excellence do so because they have, to some degree either wittingly or unwittingly, embraced biblical principles in their organizations.

> **IT IS RARE TO FIND A LEADER WHO EMBRACES THE BIBLE AS THE FOUNDATIONAL BOOK FOR BUSINESS PHILOSOPHY.**

Points to Ponder

1. List the names of five organizations that claim to be world-class, but are not. What impedes the ability of each of these organizations to deliver consistently with their claim? For each of these organizations, what changes would you recommend to enable them to deliver a world-class value proposition?

2. Based on your personal knowledge, list the names of five organizations that deliver a world-class value proposition. For each of the organizations, what is the key principle that enables the organization to deliver a world-class value proposition?

Notes

1. Michael E. Gerber, *The E-Myth Revisited* (NY: HarperBusiness, 2001), 2.

2. Ibid., 13.

3. Collins, *Good to Great*, 1–16.

4. Genesis 2:3.

5. There is debate among well-meaning Christians as to whether or not the Sabbath is a valid concept for today. It is not my purpose to argue either side of the debate; rather I am using R. G.'s conviction about the Sabbath to illustrate a point.

6. Deuteronomy 30:15–20.

Beyond Babel Model

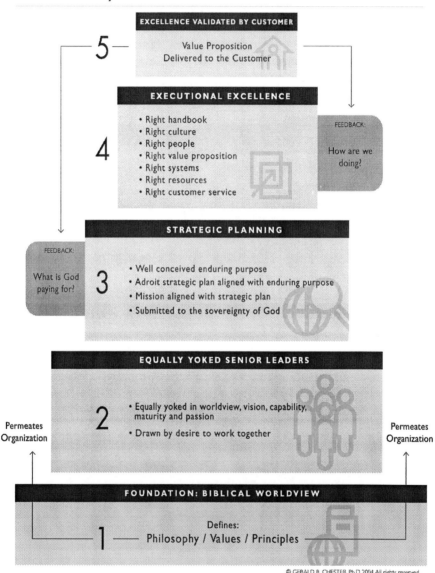

EXCELLENCE VALIDATED BY CUSTOMER

5 — Value Proposition
Delivered to the Customer

EXECUTIONAL EXCELLENCE

4
- Right handbook
- Right culture
- Right people
- Right value proposition
- Right systems
- Right resources
- Right customer service

FEEDBACK:

How are we doing?

STRATEGIC PLANNING

FEEDBACK:

What is God paying for?

3
- Well conceived enduring purpose
- Adroit strategic plan aligned with enduring purpose
- Mission aligned with strategic plan
- Submitted to the sovereignty of God

EQUALLY YOKED SENIOR LEADERS

2
- Equally yoked in worldview, vision, capability, maturity and passion
- Drawn by desire to work together

Permeates Organization

Permeates Organization

FOUNDATION: BIBLICAL WORLDVIEW

1 — Defines:
Philosophy / Values / Principles

Can You Build an
Excellent Organization?

The answer to the question, "Can you build an excellent organization?" is a conditional yes. The condition is that one must align oneself, either wittingly or unwittingly, with a biblical worldview. If the God of the Bible created the universe, one would expect to find that the principles and values found in the Bible would reveal God's intent as to how to achieve organizational excellence. If this is true, then organizations that adopt God's principles and values should experience superior blessing and success compared with those that don't.

The Beyond Babel Model is a biblically based model of organizational excellence. This model is applicable to any organization. Applying the Beyond Babel Model to any organization will serve to align that organization with a biblical worldview. The degree of alignment is proportional to the degree of prosperity, if prosperity is defined as obedience to God.

Some people intentionally seek to align their organizations with a biblical worldview. Others unknowingly and unwittingly adopt biblical principles. To the degree that they do, they are blessed.

The country of Luxembourg is an interesting case. (Note that countries are organizations just as companies and nonprofit organizations are.) This largely Roman Catholic country enjoys the highest gross domestic product per capita in the world. The reason is that the country practices certain biblical principles. Note for example:

- Though its labor force is largely union, there are no labor problems, which implies that the Golden Rule is practiced.

- Their government demonstrates financial discipline and responsibility by spending less than it takes in.

As a result of these practices, the economy enjoys stable growth, low unemployment, and low inflation. Also, the Roman Catholic worldview is socially conservative, which means that traditional Christian values are encouraged and practiced. Furthermore, the government, a family monarchy, is not encumbered with re-election concerns, so it may rule justly without fear of losing political control.

This little country illustrates the excellence that a country can achieve by practicing a few biblical values and principles.

Idolatry and Common Grace

Their deeds do not permit them to return to their God. A spirit of prostitution is in their heart; they do not acknowledge the LORD. Israel's arrogance testifies against them; the Israelites, even Ephraim, stumble in their sin; they go with their flocks and herds to seek the LORD, they will not find him; he has withdrawn himself from them.[1]

The Bible teaches that everyone worships a god. Theoretically, professing Christians worship the God of the Bible, and embrace a biblical worldview in both word and deed. Practically, though, many professing Christians embrace a biblical worldview in word but not in deed. A person who professes a biblical worldview but lives inconsistently with it is known as an actor or hypocrite.

To some degree, all Christians are hypocrites because of the impossibility to live perfectly and consistently with a biblical worldview. Nevertheless, the challenge to every Christian is to seek to walk as much as possible in the reality of a biblical worldview. Those that seek to live in the reality of a biblical worldview find increasing blessings as their alignment increasingly improves. However, those that profess a biblical worldview, but don't seek diligently to live accordingly, enjoy no more blessings than those who reject a biblical worldview. Those who reject a biblical worldview, either in word or in deed, enjoy only the blessings that non-Christians enjoy, which are the very limited blessings of common grace.

This discussion does not imply that acceptance with God is gained by works. Laboring to embrace a biblical worldview is an expression of gratitude for the gift of eternal life that is in Jesus Christ. A biblical worldview asserts that salvation is by grace. Those that have received such grace express the reality of the gift through their actions.[2]

> **LABORING TO EMBRACE A BIBLICAL WORLDVIEW IS AN EXPRESSION OF GRATITUDE FOR THE GIFT OF ETERNAL LIFE THAT IS IN JESUS CHRIST.**

Non-Christians frequently make no pretense about rejecting a biblical worldview. Rejecting a biblical worldview is tantamount to rejecting God. For example, the book of Romans clearly argues that all people have revelation about the existence and nature of God as the Creator through nature.[3] Most people are like the Old Testament nation of Israel who rejected God and then, as a result, were rejected by God.

Rejection by God is judgment. Anyone who does not accept and practice a biblical worldview is a non-Christian. Accordingly, the biblical perspective, attributed to Israel, can be applied to all non-Christians. All are idolaters and therefore God withdraws from them. Thus, non-Christians lead their organizations without the support and aide of their Creator apart from common grace.

Common grace is the grace that is common to man regardless of man's acceptance or rejection of God. God graciously provides the sun as an energy source for all mankind.[4] He sends the rain to make the harvest grow[5] and provides life and breath, indeed everything, for all mankind.[6] In many places, people live with little fear of personal safety because of the restraining work of God keeping people from manifesting the full extent of their sin.[7]

God even chooses to reveal His wisdom to fools.[8] How does God reveal His wisdom to fools who by definition reject God's revelation?[9] He does so by blessing them when they, albeit infrequently, obey some of His principles. For example, even fools seem wise when they heed God's principles regarding the use of the tongue.[10] Common grace, therefore, provides a mechanism whereby anyone can receive blessings and give blessings by simply obeying some of God's principles and embracing some of His values.

Therefore, exclusive of the grace of salvation, the doctrine of common grace, to some degree, implies that there is a correlation between obedience to God and blessings from God in a person's life regardless of the spiritual state of the person. If this correlation exists for people, it must also exist for the organizations that people create. This means that non-Christians can enjoy blessings when they run their organizations, either wittingly or unwittingly, based on some degree of alignment with biblical philosophy, principles, and values.

This was the situation with the Tower of Babel project. The project sponsors embraced some key biblical principles and enjoyed success for a time by virtue of common grace. In the end, however, the project did not endure because it was based on the wrong philosophy. The sponsors were idolaters who sought to glorify themselves instead of glorifying God, and therefore brought judgment on themselves.

Building with the Right People

"What makes for the enduring success of a company? In our view, businesses prosper when they enable individuals and society to achieve all four categories of enduring success: happiness, achievement, significance, and legacy."[11]

The above quote from an article by Laura Nash and Howard Stevenson captures the relationship between successful people and successful organizations. Organizations are simply two or more people who join together to accomplish a mission. The degree of success and excellence enjoyed by any organization is directly correlated to its people. Excellent organizations are the fruit of an excellent team. An excellent team is the fruit of excellent people. Excellent people are people who know who they are and why they are on planet Earth and are about the business of fulfilling their mission.

In Nash and Stevenson's research, they identified four key ingredients that enable any person to find success and satisfaction in life: happiness, achievement, significance, and legacy. Not surprisingly, each of these characteristics can be tied to the Bible. There is no one happier than one who is at peace with God.[12] There is no better achievement and significance than doing what one was destined to do.[13] There is no greater legacy than helping the next generation build on your achievement.[14]

> **EXCELLENT PEOPLE ARE PEOPLE WHO KNOW WHO THEY ARE AND WHY THEY ARE ON PLANET EARTH, AND ARE ABOUT THE BUSINESS OF FULFILLING THEIR MISSION.**

These four characteristics can also be connected to the C4 concept: calling, character, capability, and commissioning. Calling implies contentment and happiness because one is doing what is in one's heart. A person of noble character does not think of himself but of others. Such a person is looking for legacy opportunities to pass on knowledge and wisdom to the next generation. Capable people are high achievers and will do whatever is required to get the job done. Commissioned people know that they are significant and are content doing whatever they have been commissioned to do.

Any organization that values people and places people in the organization based on the C4 model will achieve some level of excellence. Southwest Airlines is a great example. Focusing on cultural fit, the company hires based on character and calling first, and capability second. Because of this hiring discipline, Southwest's people feel commissioned to do their jobs. Furthermore, the company has a culture of support and encouragement. The fruit of carefully selecting people is obvious. Southwest continues to be the only consistently profitable airline in the United States. By following biblical principles and hiring the right people, any organization can enjoy much success. Such is the fruit of common grace.

Building with the Right Value:
The Magic of the Golden Rule

According to Jesus, the greatest of all values is love.[15] He goes on to say that all of the commandments in the Old Testament are contained in the two commandments to love God and love our neighbor.[16] All other values emanate from love, the highest of all values. For example, honesty, integrity, mercy, and accountability are all expressions of love. Given the preeminence of love, it is not surprising to discover that organizations enjoy success when they practice the Golden Rule.

> *So in everything, do to others what you would have them do*
> *to you, for this sums up the Law and the Prophets.*[17]

The power of the Golden Rule is almost magical. Pragmatically, many companies discover that following the Golden Rule works. Organizations like Southwest Airlines, Worthington Industries, and the National Association of Realtors (NAR) recognize the Golden Rule's value and proactively practice it. Unabashedly, NAR's continuing education ethics course is built around the Golden Rule. Southwest Airlines is well known for its emphasis on valuing people. Worthington Industry's Web site states in part: "The Worthington Industries Philosophy is based on the Golden Rule—we treat our workers, customers, suppliers and shareholders as we would like to be treated."[18]

Other organizations such as FedEx, Amazon, Men's Warehouse, Lenscrafters, The Container Store, and Neiman Marcus practice the Golden Rule. Why? Because it works. By loving and, therefore, valuing people these organizations enjoy great favor with their workers, suppliers, and customers. The people quotient of the organization provides such a positive atmosphere that all stakeholders are internally compelled to go the extra mile and deliver an outstanding value proposition.

ALL OTHER VALUES EMANATE FROM LOVE.

Because of the doctrine of common grace, one doesn't have to be a professing Christian to follow the Golden Rule. Anyone can choose to. And anyone who follows it will enjoy the fruit of it. The principle of sowing and reaping works whether or not one is a Christian. The Golden Rule is about sowing seeds of blessings into people's lives. These seeds have no choice but to bear good fruit, namely, executional excellence confirmed by customers who highly value the organization's value proposition.

Common Grace Illustrated:
The Blessing of Following Biblical Principles

Notwithstanding the blessings of common grace that come to anyone who obeys God's principles, Christians have an advantage over non-Christians. Christians are able to draw on the power of the Holy Spirit and, therefore, practice the Golden Rule and all of God's principles better than non-Christians. If life is a holistic blend of physical and spiritual reality defined by the Creator through the Bible, Christians are in the best position to efficaciously live life.

Non-Christians live primarily in the physical world with, at best, minimal understanding of the spiritual world. Those who choose to embrace a spiritual component of reality, but reject a biblical worldview, live in deception. Hence, Christians enjoy the position of communion with the God of Creation who can guide them into all truth. Despite the deception of non-Christians, common grace still affords them some level of blessings if they choose, either wittingly or unwittingly, to obey God's principles.

A July 2001 article in *Fortune* called "God and Business"[19] illustrates how non-Christians can enjoy blessings by means of common grace. This article provides case studies involving six people, each with different worldviews and practicing different spiritual principles. In the table below, each spiritual principle is noted and a biblical perspective provided. Despite the fact that each case study highlights a spiritual principle that when practiced provides blessings by means of common grace, only the case study of the management consultant lines up with biblical Christianity.

> IF LIFE IS A HOLISTIC BLEND OF PHYSICAL AND SPIRITUAL REALITY DEFINED BY THE CREATOR THROUGH THE BIBLE, CHRISTIANS ARE IN THE BEST POSITION TO EFFICACIOUSLY LIVE LIFE.

CASE STUDY	PRODUCT/ SERVICE	WORLDVIEW	KEY SPIRITUAL PRINCIPLE	BIBLICAL PERSPECTIVE
R.C. Wiley Home Furnishings	Retail Furniture	Mormon	Observing the Sabbath.	Following biblical principles leads to blessings.
Management Consultant	M&A Services	Protestant Christian	Work for God, avoid the seduction of money and power.	Fairly well aligned with Scripture.
Lawyer	Legal Services	Buddhist	Vipassana meditation.	Meditation is a fruitful excercise particularly when one meditates on Scripture.
Greyston Bakery	Gourmet brownies, cakes, & tarts	Buddhist/ Christian Universalist	Everyone deserves a chance, but each is responsible for his or her actions. The company seeks to take care of its workers and supports people pursuing their own path.	Valuing people is very biblical. Universalism is a big temptation as it seems to embrace all. Christianity is not syncretistic.
Catalytica	Pharmaceuticals and Energy	Jewish	Spiritual, but not connected to a synagogue. Uses meditation to help love others and gain discernment for making decisions.	Life is more than tangible reality. Practicing the Golden Rule and listening to your intuition can do nothing but help. However, not living in community will limit one's ability to find creative solutions.
Blistex	Lip-Care Products	Catholic Christian	Values people and leads by working for them.	While valuing people is clearly biblical, being out of balance by excessively valuing people over stewardship could lead to blocking people from their destiny and poor financial performance.

Although the other case studies provided some benefit for the respective practitioners, the underlying worldviews were inaccurate, which means that the principles provide limited blessings, by virtue of common grace, to the practitioners. For example, the

Buddhist practice of meditation is a very helpful spiritual practice and is consistent with principles taught in the Bible.[20] However, the Buddhist worldview does not embrace the saving work of Jesus Christ in accordance with a biblical worldview. Therefore, Buddhism is inconsistent with a biblical worldview, which means that practitioners of Buddhism will not enjoy the blessings of eternal life that come uniquely through Jesus Christ.

Despite the limited blessings of common grace, only a biblical worldview provides the philosophy, principles, and values that are fully efficacious both personally and organizationally. A biblical worldview addresses all of life and answers the questions in the human heart regarding meaning, purpose, and significance. Only a biblical worldview provides direction and guidance as to what man is to do now and what he will do in eternity. Therefore, only a biblical worldview will be fully efficacious to help practitioners achieve personal and organizational excellence.

Conclusion

Can you build an excellent organization? Anyone can choose to follow the principles of organizational excellence defined by the Creator of the universe. Everyone, however, worships something. The worship of any god other than the God of the Bible is idolatry. Idolatry defines the worldview and, therefore, the principles and practices of the person and/or organization worshipping that idol. It is axiomatic that idolatry and biblical worldview are mutually exclusive; hence, individuals and organizations that practice idolatry cannot achieve a high level of either individual or organizational excellence. Nevertheless, organizations that pragmatically discover biblical principles, such as generosity and personal destiny, are blessed by means of common grace when they practice these principles.

Even following only one biblical principle, such as the Golden Rule, can provide great benefit to the practitioner. But there is another level of operational excellence for those who more fully embrace a biblical worldview as the underlying definer of organizational policy and practice. Organizations that seek to fully integrate a biblical worldview enjoy not only a vast source of principles and methodologies that can be gleaned from the Bible, but also the leading of the Holy Spirit who will guide them into all truth.

Can you build an excellent organization? Common grace provides a vehicle of limited blessings for any organization. True excellence, however, defined as obedience to God, can only be enjoyed by organizations that fully seek to integrate a biblical worldview and obedience to the Holy Spirit into the philosophy and practice of the organization.

Points to Ponder

1. List five examples of how common grace positively impacts your life every day.

2. What would the business environment be like if God withheld common grace and the Golden Rule was not practiced?

3. According to Jesus, what are the two greatest commandments? How is the Golden Rule related to these commandments?

4. List the names of five organizations that you personally know that do not consistently practice the Golden Rule. Describe your experience with these organizations.

5. List the names of five organizations that you personally know that consistently practice the Golden Rule. Describe your experience with these organizations.

Notes

1. Hosea 5:4–6.

2. James 2:14–26.

3. Romans 1:20–23.

4. Matthew 5:45.

5. Acts 14:15–17.

6. Acts 17:25.

7. 2 Thessalonians 2:6–7.

8. Proverbs 14:33.

9. Proverbs 1:7ff.

10. Proverbs 17:28.

11. Laura Nash and Howard Stevenson, "Success That Lasts," *Harvard Business Review*, February 2004, 102–109.

12. Philippians 4:4–7.

13. Ephesians 2:10, John 17 (especially vs. 4).

14. Proverbs 13:22.

15. Matthew 22:36–40.

16. Ibid.

17. Matthew 7:12.

18. http://www.worthingtonindustries.com

19. Marc Gunther, "God and Business," *Fortune*, 9 July 2001, 59–80.

20. Psalms 19:14.

Beyond Babel Model

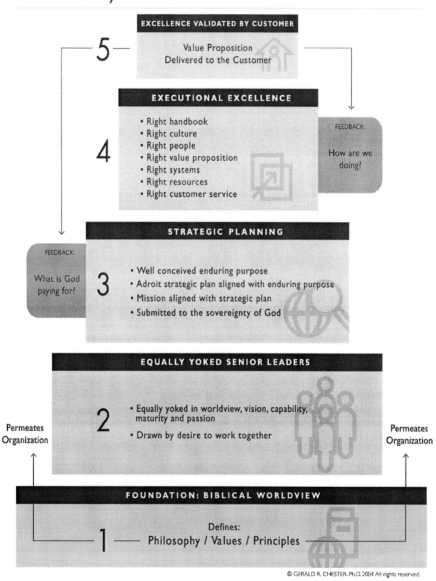

5

EXCELLENCE VALIDATED BY CUSTOMER

Value Proposition
Delivered to the Customer

4

EXECUTIONAL EXCELLENCE

- Right handbook
- Right culture
- Right people
- Right value proposition
- Right systems
- Right resources
- Right customer service

FEEDBACK:

How are we doing?

3

STRATEGIC PLANNING

- Well conceived enduring purpose
- Adroit strategic plan aligned with enduring purpose
- Mission aligned with strategic plan
- Submitted to the sovereignty of God

FEEDBACK:

What is God paying for?

2

EQUALLY YOKED SENIOR LEADERS

- Equally yoked in worldview, vision, capability, maturity and passion
- Drawn by desire to work together

Permeates Organization

Permeates Organization

1

FOUNDATION: BIBLICAL WORLDVIEW

Defines:
Philosophy / Values / Principles

In Summary

The biblical story of the Tower of Babel is an interesting study in organizational behavior. The members of that organization used three key principles and attained a level of success. First, the leaders developed unity of purpose. Second, they developed a well conceived strategic plan built on finding a good location to build on and used the appropriate building materials. And third, they executed well by working as a team with personal agendas submitted to the good of the whole. Using these three key principles, which are included in the Beyond Babel Model, they enjoyed temporary success. Their downfall, however, was that they didn't embrace the whole model. The missing element was a complete biblical worldview. The lack of a biblical worldview meant that they did not seek God's will on the project and built it based on a purpose that was not aligned with God. Despite apparent short-term success, such presumption was doomed to failure.

The purpose of this book is to challenge organizations to go beyond Babel. By this I mean that organizations must embrace the full application of a biblical worldview. By doing this, organizations will function based on alignment with God and His purposes. This is the foundation of excellence that leads to enduring blessings. From this foundation, the other key elements of the Beyond Babel Model flow: unified senior leaders, strategic planning, execution excellence, and customer validation. The foundation of a biblical worldview provides an organization its philosophy, values, and principles that permeate the organization and provide the direction needed to carry out God's purpose for the organization. Only then will the organization be able to move beyond Babel.

Sadly, most organizations have little understanding of the critical role that a biblical worldview plays in laying the requisite foundation for enduring organizational success. For most organizations, there is a dearth of understanding concerning the role a philosophical base plays in every decision and action. Pundits in organizational behavior focus their attention on empirical studies, which largely seek to identify key operating practices with little understanding of the philosophy that drives these practices. As a result, the conclusions from the research to date are incomplete. While such research provides valuable insight and contributes to the discussion, no studies recognize the critical importance of a philosophical foundation. The focus of the research tends to be on the practical application of the principles that are pragmatically discerned by empirical studies.

Clearly, this approach plays well with organizational leaders who tend to be pragmatic themselves. But pragmatism, as a philosophical foundation, is not satisfying to anyone who wishes to embrace a holistic view of reality. The objective of this book, therefore, is to illustrate how a biblical worldview uniquely provides the philosophy, values, and principles needed to achieve enduring organizational excellence.

The Beyond Babel Model

If you agree with the presuppositions of the book and logic presented above, I submit to you the following building blocks to achieve organizational excellence.

1. Biblical Worldview

A biblical worldview is the only valid worldview. As such it is the essential starting point to define the values and principles that organizations must embrace to achieve excellence. A biblical worldview provides perspective on finance, people, success, communication, teamwork, selling, leadership, management, planning, and so forth. Most organizations pragmatically discover and unwittingly adopt biblical principles and values. This explains why many organizations enjoy some level of enduring success. However, to enjoy the highest level of success, organizations must not only adopt biblical principles, but must also embrace the work, power, and guidance of the Holy Spirit. Jesus sent the Holy Spirit to those who believe in Him to guide us into all truth.[1]

2. Equally Yoked Senior Leader

No organization can achieve excellence without leadership that is equally yoked. There are many facets to equal yoking. The starting point is a biblical worldview, which provides common principles and values from which to build the culture of the organization. In addition, the senior leaders need to be comparable in maturity and strength of gifting. Also, there needs to be a diverse blend of complementary skills needed to effectively lead the organization. From this foundation of unity and diversity, adroit senior leaders develop creative strategic plans to guide the organization into a compelling world-class value proposition.

3. Strategic Planning

Strategic planning provides the focus and boundaries within which an organization functions. No organization can be all things to all people. Every organization must find its niche, the place where it can produce a world-class value proposition. Only in this place will the organization truly thrive.

4. Executional Excellence

This is the focus of most empirical studies of organizational excellence. The tactical execution of the strategic plan is the daily work of every organization. It is where the rubber meets the road, the "how to" that must be done to deliver an outstanding value proposition. The direction for any great organization comes from the strategic plan. A biblical worldview provides the principles and values that shape and define the culture, systems, and practices of the organization. To some degree, the level of excellence achieved by an organization is a measure of how well the organization is aligned with a biblical worldview, how equally yoked the leaders are, and how well conceived the strategic plan is.

5. Validation by Customers

The ultimate test of any value proposition is the customer. Organizations exist to serve customers; therefore, it is imperative that organizations understand the needs of their customers. Validation by customers must be a priority in any organization seeking to produce world-class results. No one sees all the perspectives and no one sees himself or herself well. The independent validation by third parties is vital to seeing reality and making the appropriate course corrections.

The Beyond Babel Model of organizational excellence rests squarely and firmly on a biblical worldview. This provides a perspective on reality, as well as values and principles that will bring blessings to any organization by enabling it to deliver a world-class value proposition.

A biblical worldview also includes an understanding of the role of the intangible world. For many, the idea that organizational activity has an intangible component is an oxymoron. Yet, all of us have experienced situations and events that cannot be explained by reason or logic. The biblical worldview offers an explanation: the spirit world. In this world, there is a struggle between good and evil just as in the tangible world. In some way, however, the intangible is linked to the tangible.

This link between the intangible and tangible gives Christians an advantage because they realize its existence and have the power of the Holy Spirit available to them for wisdom and guidance. What a marvelous experience it would be to see an organization operating on a biblical worldview tapped into the power of the Holy Spirit. This would redefine the meaning of a world-class organization.

What About Individuals?

How could one go wrong basing one's life on a biblical worldview? With this foundation, one is equipped to discover one's life purpose. If indeed the God of creation is purposeful, then each human being has a reason for living. A logical corollary is that each of us should be about finding the reason that God made us and doing whatever we were meant to do.

Agnostic scholar Charles Murray wrote a book titled *Human Accomplishment* in which he sought to understand why human achievement is not evenly distributed across all cultures. Going back through the past three thousand years of human history, Murray sought to understand what enabled human achievement. His surprising conclusion[2] was that Christianity (biblical worldview) underlies virtually all human achievement. In particular, Murray stated that the paradigm of Christianity that supports human accomplishment consisted of three main points:

- One's life has a purpose.

- The main function of life is to find one's purpose and do it.

- One's efforts to fulfill one's purpose are efficacious.

These were amazing conclusions coming from a scholar who rejected a biblical worldview but was bound by honesty to his research to conclude that a biblical worldview undergirded virtually all human achievement.

If, indeed, each of us has a purpose, our function on earth is to fulfill that purpose and our efforts to do so can be efficacious, what does this imply about organizational excellence? Does not this suggest that excellent organizations need people who are walking in their individual destinies? This simply means that each person in the organization has C4 to do the job that he or she is doing. How could an organization so populated not be a world-class organization? An organization with every person in the right spot would be overwhelmingly productive, efficient, effective, customer sensitive, equally yoked, strategically aligned, and profitable. This would be world-class.

No organization can begin to accomplish this without starting with a biblical worldview. Only a biblical worldview provides the correct perspective, principles, and values to build such an organization. Furthermore, only a biblical worldview provides the basis for equally yoked senior leaders who are knit together with the same philosophy, values, and principles. Only leaders like this can be sensitive to the Holy Spirit in developing the organization's strategic plan. Only organizations with deft strategic plans can execute the delivery of excellent value propositions because of the culture, people, practices, philosophy, principles, values, and systems that are defined and undergirded by a biblical worldview. Only excellent value propositions receive enduring validation by customers.

So do individuals count? By all means, they are at the heart of making organizations excellent.

Final Thought

Thank you for persevering through this book. I know it was not easy, but I hope you were blessed as you wrestled with the concepts. Clearly, they are challenging because most of us have not been taught to think about organizations from a biblical worldview. Whether you learned about business in school or on the job, you probably learned man's way of doing business, not God's way. The common perspective is that God is not concerned with physical matters, such as business and organizational problems; He is focused on spiritual matters. In reality, God created the physical universe and called it good. He then created man to rule it by reflecting His glory. God is concerned, therefore, about both spiritual and physical reality. It is seamless to Him.

GOD IS CONCERNED ABOUT BOTH SPIRITUAL AND PHYSICAL REALITY.

This book presents a biblical model for organizational excellence. The Beyond Babel Model challenges us to glorify God by building organizations based on biblical philosophy, values, and principles. The enduring success that any organization enjoys is directly related to its alignment with God and His purposes. There seems to be little understanding of this reality and, therefore, a dearth of truly excellent organizations.

Most organizations enjoy the simple and limited blessings of common grace. Common grace is a wonderful gift from God and enables us to live safely and comfortably in many places of the world. Organizations that follow some limited number of biblical principles are better and more successful, by any definition, than those that embrace almost no biblical principles. By practicing biblical principles, organizations can enjoy limited success comparable to Babel, but cannot move beyond Babel because their purposes do not line up with God's purposes.

Organizations that embrace a biblical worldview and seek to walk it out by the leading of the Holy Spirit have unlimited potential for blessings to all. Only by living this way, will God's enduring favor rain on those who choose to embrace His perspective. The truly excellent organizations will be those who are deeply devoted to living out the reality of a biblical worldview in the power of the Holy Spirit, not out of duty, but out of deep gratitude for the gift of eternal life through Jesus Christ. From those who know the depth of God's gift to them, a well of thankfulness overflows into a heart of obedience. Men and women so motivated become the key leaders in organizations that fanatically embrace and practice a biblical worldview. Only with such leaders can organizations move beyond Babel. To go beyond Babel, an organization must practice biblical principles in the power of the Holy Spirit consistent with God's purposes.

I would love to interact with you as you seek to apply biblical principles to your personal life and to your organization. Appendix I provides a list of frequently asked questions to stimulate your thinking, and also a means of communicating with me.

I hope this treatise will encourage many to consider the reality that the God of the Bible does care about organizations and how they operate. He cares enough to give us many principles and values that will enable organizations to achieve greatness. Can we get a vision for what this looks like and begin to walk in it? I pray we can.

Notes

1. John 16:13.
2. Susan Olasky, "Gaining Ground," *World*, 10 January 2004.

20 Frequently Asked Questions (FAQs)

1. How does a management team begin to apply the Beyond Babel Model to their organization?

2. What should I do if no one else on the management team embraces the model?

3. How do I determine an organization's worldview?

4. Which is the most important of the C4 elements? Why?

5. How do you define a Christian and a non-Christian?

6. Should I hire a non-Christian?

7. Should I hire someone just because he or she professes to be a Christian?

8. Should I work for someone who does not have C4 for his or her position?

9. What should I do if I don't have C4 for my position?

10. What is truth?

11. What should I do if I am a member of an unequally yoked team?

12. How do I determine my organization's value proposition?

13. What does *prosperity* mean?

14. Why do the wicked prosper?

15. How does the Great Commission (Matthew 28:18-20) relate to the Divine Mandate (Genesis 1:26-28)?

16. Does sin nullify the Divine Mandate?

17. Does God equally value the spiritual and physical dimensions of reality?

18. Does God give us strategic plans to solve problems in the spiritual and physical dimensions?

19. What do the actions of Jesus in expelling the merchants from the temple say about His view of business (Matthew 21:12-13)?

20. Does the Beyond Babel Model work for screening investment opportunities?

For answers to these and other FAQs, please go to the Web site www.strategieswork.com.

Please send any other questions you have to info@strategieswork.com.

Appendix II
More Comparisons

In this Appendix, some of the research projects that purport to discover the axioms that facilitate organizational excellence are compared to the Beyond Babel Model. Generally, researchers heuristically and pragmatically discover the principles that they articulate with little understanding that the principles can be found in the Bible. The Beyond Babel Model embraces the assumption that God, as the Creator of the universe, revealed in the Bible the philosophy, values, and principles that He wishes organizations to practice. Furthermore, it is assumed that organizational excellence can only be achieved through embracing God's philosophy, values, and principles of organizational behavior. Therefore the degree of excellence enjoyed by any organization is the degree to which the organization is aligned with God's philosophy, principles, and values.

As far as I know, the Beyond Babel Model is the only model of organizational excellence that is purposely rooted in a biblical worldview. If my assumptions are correct, the results of the various empirical studies are nothing more than subsets of the Beyond Babel Model.

The following is a discussion of some of the various models. The purpose of the discussion is to demonstrate that the empirical studies can be tied to the Beyond Babel Model and therefore viewed as subsets of the model.

Built to Last

Prior to writing *Good to Great*, Jim Collins partnered with Jerry Porras to write *Built to Last*.[1] In this book, the authors were seeking to understand the principles that enable organizations, widely admired by their peers, to make sustained long-term contributions to the world. This book seeks to uncover principles that facilitate enduring excellence. Based on their research, the authors posit eight key principles that facilitate developing enduring organizational excellence. Not surprisingly, each of these principles can be found in the Beyond Babel Model (see Diagram 9).

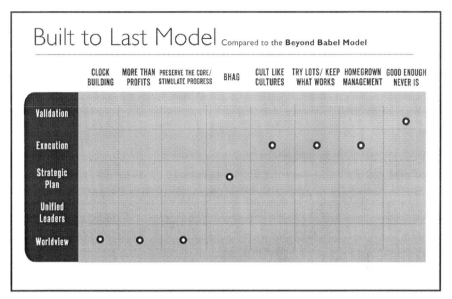

	CLOCK BUILDING	MORE THAN PROFITS	PRESERVE THE CORE/ STIMULATE PROGRESS	BHAG	CULT LIKE CULTURES	TRY LOTS/ KEEP WHAT WORKS	HOMEGROWN MANAGEMENT	GOOD ENOUGH NEVER IS
Validation								o
Execution					o	o	o	
Strategic Plan				o				
Unified Leaders								
Worldview	o	o	o					

Diagram 9

1. Clock Building, Not Time Telling

This principle refers to the question that every management team must answer: What kind of organization am I going to build? There are only two choices: either a single-generational organization or a multigenerational organization. Collins and Porras call a single-generational organization time telling. This type of organization is built around a great idea, concept, or personality. In other words, the organization is strongly dependent on a key person, product, or technology.

When a better idea or concept comes around or the personality passes on, the organization does not endure. On the other hand, clock building refers to multigenerational organizations. If a clock is built, anyone can tell the time; a time teller is not required. These organizations are built on an enduring purpose that transcends concepts, ideas, and personalities. The concept of a multigenerational organization is rooted in a biblical worldview and is commonly known as generational transfer.

2. More than Profits

Enduring organizations view profit as a by-product of excellent performance. These organizations are driven by a timeless purpose and value system. The actual product or service delivered by the organization will change with time, but the core ideology (unchanging purpose and values), never changes. Profit is certainly a necessary ingredient to success but it is not the driving force.

This principle is consistent with a biblical worldview that teaches that God created man for a purpose and that money is not a goal but the fruit of faithful stewardship. Furthermore, the Bible articulates a value system rooted in values such as love, truth, honesty, integrity, humility, perseverance, excellence, teamwork, accountability, selflessness, mercy, kindness, faithfulness, dependability, loyalty, and tenacity.

3. Preserve the Core While Simulating Progress

Enduring great organizations possess immutable core ideology, enduring purpose and values, without impeding the creativity and progress of the organization. The twin organizational absolutes of enduring purpose and values are consistent with a biblical worldview that articulates both the purpose of mankind to rule creation by multiplying and subduing, and to reflect the glory of God by practicing principles, methodologies, and values consistent with biblical teaching.

4. Big Hairy Audacious Goals (BHAG)

A BHAG is a mechanism to bring focus to an organization. It is an energizing, engaging statement that articulates what an organization wishes to accomplish. By its very nature it tends to be overwhelming, but when widely embraced by members of the organization, it brings sharp focus and strategic alignment.

In the Beyond Babel Model, the BHAG is one of the products of wise strategic planning. Building on the core purpose and values of the organization, the strategic planning process should ferret out the extraneous and distracting ideas to bring the organization to clear and sharp focus. A BHAG is a statement that encapsulates this focus with eye-popping and heart-stopping power. The sheer power of the BHAG statement provides an organization with compelling strategic focus and boundaries.

5. Cultlike Cultures

An organization is simply a group of people who join together to accomplish a mission. For an organization to achieve maximum effectiveness, it must have everyone in the right position with the right attitude. Like a professional sports team that wins a championship, every person on the team must be highly skilled and motivated to win the game. Cultlike cultures are unified, focused, and fanatical about achieving the organization's goals. Such cultures are the natural product of an organization practicing the Beyond Babel Model. These organizations display unity, focus, and fanatical commitment to providing a world-class value proposition in the context of a biblical worldview.

6. Try a Lot of Stuff and Keep What Works

Despite man's advancement in understanding the laws of nature, we can only solve the simplest of problems. As a result, most advances happen heuristically. Given this reality, excellent organizations recognize the need to experiment. Such organizations encourage creativity and risk taking, not foolishly, but prudently. In the Beyond Babel Model, a culture rooted in a biblical worldview invites innovation and progress. Mistakes are viewed as the natural consequence of such activities and are not penalized, but are used as learning experiences.

7. Homegrown Management

The best way for an organization to build management is through internal growth. Such managers tend to know the heartbeat of the organization, understand its culture, and are very loyal. In the Beyond Babel Model, excellent execution happens when an equally yoked management team that is working to disciple other managers leads an organization. Such mentoring provides an organization with a stable of management talent that will facilitate long-term excellent performance.

8. Good Enough Never Is

The world is always changing. No organization can stand still or be content. If it tries, it will go backward. Any organization that perceives of itself as good runs the risk of becoming content. Being content led the railroads in the early twentieth century to fall from the pinnacle of business leadership. The reason is simple. The railroads did not realize that they were in the transportation business; hence, they were content to run railroads. Thus, when better technology came, they did not recognize the implications. Truly great organizations are never content. They are always seeking input from customers to find ways to improve. This principle is expressed in the fifth building block of the Beyond Babel Model—customer validation.

The principles pragmatically discovered by the authors of *Built to Last* are consistent with the Beyond Babel Model. The reason is simple: organizational excellence is the fruit of alignment with biblical truth, which is the foundation of the model.

In Search of Excellence

In Search of Excellence (Search), the original empirical study that sought to understand the principles that facilitate organizational excellence, was written in the early 1980s.[2] One of the authors, Tom Peters, later confessed to faking the data; that is, the selection of companies was not scientifically determined. Furthermore, Peters acknowledged that the study was biased by his own jaundiced perspective.[3] Nevertheless, I have included it because Peters did gather considerable data and his conclusions are worth noting.

Search posits eight attributes of excellent organizations. As with the other empirical models, each attribute can be found in the Beyond Babel Model (see Diagram 10).

1. A Bias for Action

Organizations are either proactive or reactive. Proactive organizations are willing to take risks and try new ideas. There is no fear of failure since failure is viewed as a tool to help improve the organization. Having a bias for action is an attribute that permeates excellent organizations. It is readily seen in the execution or implementation of the value proposition and is a key ingredient of good stewardship. In the Beyond Babel Model, a proactive culture is required to facilitate the fourth building block—executional excellence.

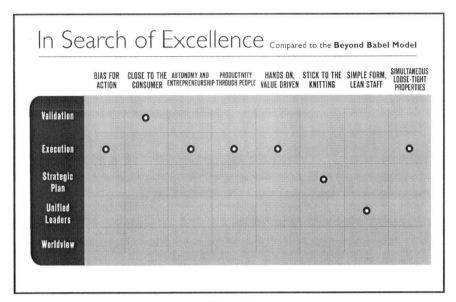

Diagram 10

2. Close to the Customer

No organization can make good decisions regarding its value proposition without customer feedback. Anyone or any organization that attempts to make critical choices without customer input is guilty of extreme hubris. Such organizations are doomed to mediocrity at best and failure at worse. The attribute of being close to the customer is contained in the fifth building block of the Beyond Babel Model. Furthermore, organizations that seek to know and respond to customers are practicing the value of humility.

3. Autonomy and Entrepreneurship

Each human being is uniquely gifted. Wise leaders recognize the gifting in others and create environments that facilitate and encourage people to be creative and take calculated risks. When this happens, the organization releases power to solve problems and develop new ideas. The fourth key to organizational excellence is executional excellence. Embracing the diversity of gifting in people is a critical element for achieving executional excellence. No organization can achieve world-class status without a skillful blend of people working in concert to deliver the organization's value proposition.

4. Productivity Through People

No organization can accomplish anything without people. Leadership is not enough. Leaders must have someone to lead, someone that will execute the plan of the leaders and execute it well. For people to execute well, they need to feel valued. Excellent organizations have environments or cultures that value people. Valued people feel significant. When they feel significant, they work with purpose to deliver an excellent value proposition. Clearly, this is a key ingredient of executional excellence, the fourth building block of the Beyond Babel Model.

5. Hands On, Value Driven

Great organizations have great managers, leaders who connect with the people. These managers inspect what they expect, not in an autocratic manner but as servant leaders, that is, leaders who seek to serve rather than dictate. This style of leadership is critical for delivering a world-class value proposition and is a key component of executional excellence, the fourth building block of the Beyond Babel Model.

6. Stick to the Knitting

No organization is all things to all people. Every organization must determine its focus. This is the role of strategic planning. The management team of each world-class organization must define, with cogent clarity, the value proposition and the plan for delivering the value proposition. Focus is a salient characteristic of adroit strategic planning, the third building block of the Beyond Babel Model.

7. Simple Form, Lean Staff

Complexity seems to be the handmaiden of confusion. Organizations that adopt complex structures and large staffs tend to bog down in bureaucracy. Great organizations are lean and nimble. Great management teams are flexible and sensitive. They are generally slightly understaffed and avoid bureaucratic tendencies with a passion because they understand the critical need to be continually adjusting to market conditions. The second building block of the Beyond Babel Model is senior leaders who are unified and equally yoked; hence, they are lean and efficient.

8. Simultaneous Loose-Tight Properties

The irony of embracing seemingly conflicting values does not sway great organizations, but rather it empowers them. For example, holding mercy in balance with accountability is a key element of delivering the value proposition in a world-class manner. Extreme mercy leads to dysfunction and extreme accountability breeds tyranny. Neither works by itself without the balance brought by the other. Great organizations understand the critical need for such balance. Executional excellence, the fourth building block of the Beyond Babel Model, requires the flexibility to balance seemingly contradictory values in a way that delivers the value proposition in a world-class manner.

Search does not include an attribute associated with principles or values, though each of the attributes are clearly connected to the underlying philosophy of the organization. Neither is there any reference to the underlying worldview of the organizations studied; however, the authors do note that many of the organizations have strong unchanging core values and principles.

As with the other empirical studies of excellent organizations, the attributes delineated in *Search* can be found within the Beyond Babel Model. As with most of the other studies, the emphasis on the articulated attributes tends to be on executional excellence, the fourth building block of the Beyond Babel Model. This is not surprising as most business leaders tend to be no-nonsense, pragmatic people; hence, the writers have simply played to their audience.

Natural Church Development

Some of the most common organizations today are churches. The world is rife with churches of all types. Christian Schwarz conducted a research study to determine the attributes of healthy, growing churches. The results of his study were compiled in the book *Natural Church Development* (NCD).[4] As with other empirical studies seeking to determine the characteristics of excellent organizations, he articulates a set of attributes that he claims are keys to healthy, growing churches. Despite the fact that many view churches differently from other organizations, there is really very little difference. Every organization is simply two or more people who have come together to

NCD Model Compared to the **Beyond Babel Model**

	EMPOWERING LEADERSHIP	GIFT-ORIENTED MINISTRY	PASSIONATE SPIRITUALITY	FUNCTIONAL STRUCTURES	INSPIRING WORSHIP	HOLISTIC SMALL GROUPS	NEED ORIENTED EVANGELISM	LOVING RELATIONSHIPS
Validation	An annual survey of key members of the church is used to identify strengths and weaknesses.							
Execution	o	o	o	o	o	o	o
Strategic Plan								
Unified Leaders	o							
Worldview								

Diagram 11

accomplish a mission; therefore, one can glean principles from this study that will apply to any organization. Furthermore and not surprisingly, each of the NCD attributes can be found in the Beyond Babel Model (see Diagram 11).

1. Empowered Leadership

Uncommissioned leadership is unempowered leadership. To be world-class, an organization must have world-class leadership. This requires leaders who have C4 to lead the organization. The fourth component of C4 is commissioning. An organization must commission its leaders; otherwise the leaders will feel insecure and, therefore, be ineffective. The second building block of the Beyond Babel Model is equally yoked senior leaders, leaders who have C4 and have the freedom to lead with confidence that they will be supported.

2. Gift-Oriented Ministry

This attribute simply recognizes the C4 of each person in the organization and uses each person accordingly. No organization can achieve executional excellence without having the right people in the right positions.

3. Passionate Spirituality

The first component of C4 is calling. Calling speaks of one's heart or passion. When people do what they have a passion to do, then work is not work. To be world class at delivering the value proposition of the organization requires that everyone in the organization does what he or she has a passion to do.

4. Functional Structures

Every organization has to have structure. The best organizations tend to have as little structure as possible, but what they do have facilitates the delivery of the value proposition rather than impeding it. Executional excellence requires the appropriate structure and systems to support the adroit delivery of the value proposition.

5. Inspiring Worship

The Bible instructs us to work as if working for the Lord.[5] From a biblical worldview, delivering an outstanding value proposition is an act of worship. Clearly, such perspective is rooted in the worldview of the organization, but it is fully expressed in the executional excellence displayed in the delivery of the value proposition.

6. Holistic Small Groups

Great organizations tend to break work down into teams. Every person in an organization is then part of one or more small groups that can provide support, guidance, and accountability. These small groups serve as small communities that give people the sense of belonging. Everyone wants to find his or her place and fit into that place. When people find their team, great things begin to happen. Specifically, the organization begins to execute with excellence and to deliver an outstanding value proposition.

7. Need-Oriented Evangelism

This is simply sales. Every organization must be about selling its value proposition. As the old adage goes, nothing happens until someone sells something. World-class organizations work hard to understand the needs of the customers and then shape the value proposition accordingly. Meeting the true needs of the customers is the heart of executional excellence.

8. Loving Relationships

People in every organization require tender loving care. No one works well under tyranny and abuse. Superior organizations understand this reality and seek to provide a sensitive, caring environment that values people and encourages them to find their place. As with so many of the other attributes, this one is a key element to facilitate executional excellence.

The NCD model lines up with the Beyond Babel Model. Seven of the eight attributes are corollaries of executional excellence, the fourth building block of the Beyond Babel Model. As is true of most empirical studies, the focus is on the operating practices, not the underlying philosophy that defines the principles and values of the organization. The philosophy, or worldview, of an organization is the foundation from which everything else emanates. It defines the organization's philosophical yoke to which each person needs to subscribe. It provides definition as to how the organization views success. It undergirds the strategic planning process. And it provides the culture, values, and principles by which the organization operates. Sadly, most researchers fail to understand the critical role of worldview in providing the foundation for organizational excellence. But given the propensity to organizational pragmatism, it is not surprising that the researchers would be looking for practical attributes and overlook the root from which these attributes come.

Steps to Influence

Church pastor James Ryle teaches an eight-step process that will lead any person or organization to a place of influence.[6] In his linear process, each step is a predicate for the next. Not surprisingly each step is a biblical value or principle. The process begins with vision. Vision leads to unity. People unite based on a vision or common worldview about something. Unity leads to relationship. A relationship that people enjoy is based on the unifying common vision. Relationship leads to communication. Communication is rooted in the unifying common vision that provides the basis of the relationship. Communication facilitates building commitment to the vision. Commitment releases creativity as to how to realize the vision. Creativity opens the door for excellence. And excellence paves the way for influence.

Excellence is a value that is respected and esteemed by all. Anyone who wants to be really good at anything wants to learn from the best. Likewise, organizations that desire to achieve excellence seek to learn the principles that enable other organizations to achieve greatness.

VISION ▶ UNITY ▶ RELATIONSHIP ▶ COMMUNICATION ▶ COMMITMENT ▶ CREATIVITY ▶ EXCELLENCE ▶ INFLUENCE

Comparing these "steps to influence," it is easy to see that they fit into the Beyond Babel Model (see Diagram 12). Vision is the heart of a strategic plan. Unity and relationship are essential characteristics of senior leaders. Communication and commitment should be the fruit of a well-conceived strategic plan. Creativity and excellence should be characteristics of the execution of the strategic plan. The result of the process is that customers validate the value proposition by being influenced. The test of a truly excellent organization is sustained influence whereby customers embrace the value proposition and encourage others to do so as well.

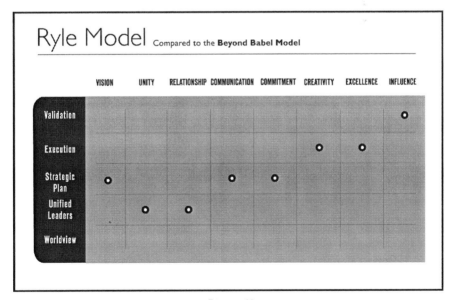

Diagram 12

The Malcolm Baldrige Criteria for Excellence

Since the late 1980s, the federal goverment has sought to encourage organizational excellence through the annual Malcolm Baldrige Award. This award is given based on compliance with what are perceived to be the best practices in seven different categories. According to the National Institute of Standards and Technology Web site on March 4, 2004,[7] candidates for the award are evaluated based on the following criteria:

I. Leadership

Examines how senior executives guide the organization and how the organization addresses its responsibilities to the public and practices good citizenship.

2. Strategic Planning

Examines how the organization sets strategic directions and how it determines key action plans.

3. Customer and Market Focus

Examines how the organization determines requirements and expectations of customers and markets; builds relationships with customers; and acquires, satisfies, and retains customers.

4. Measurement, Analysis, and Knowledge Management

Examines the management, effective use, analysis, and improvement of data and information to support key organization processes and the organization's performance management system.

5. Human Resource Focus

Examines how the organization enables its workforce to develop its full potential and how the workforce is aligned with the organization's objectives.

6. Process Management

Examines aspects of how key production, delivery, and support processes are designed, managed, and improved.

7. Business Results

Examines the organization's performance and improvement in its key business areas: customer satisfaction, financial and workplace performance, human resources, supplier and partner performance, operational performance, and governance and social responsibility. The category also examines how the organization performs relative to competitors.

The correlation of the Baldrige criteria to the Beyond Babel Model is easy (see Diagram 13). The first three Baldrige criteria map, respectively, to the second (equally yoked senior leaders), third (strategic planning), and fifth (customer validation) building blocks of the Beyond Babel Model. The next three criteria map to the fourth building block (executional excellence). And the last criterion maps to the fifth building block (customer validation). Noticeably missing from the Baldrige model is the first building block (worldview). This reflects a lack of understanding of the philosophical basis. Underlying every value or principle is a worldview that provides the conceptual basis for one to accept the value or principle as worthy of emulation.

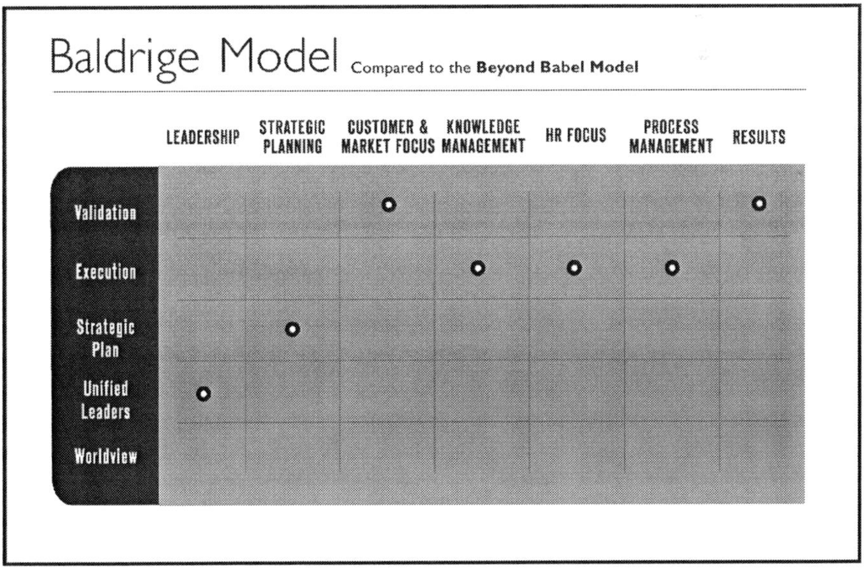

Diagram 13

Remember my client who believed that good business was not paying bills before the vendors threatened to cut off services or sue him? He did not value his credit rating or reputation. To him this was the best practice. What is the basis for differing with him? Clearly, it must be based on a different philosophy or worldview. Ultimately, the root of everyone's thinking is a belief system that leads to a worldview.

Worldview is the basis for defining one's values and principles. Based on one's values and principles, one can define the best practices—the practices that lead to the desired results consistent with one's values and principles. Therefore the foundation for any model of organizational excellence must be a philosophy or a worldview. This book asserts that only a biblical worldview will lead to enduring organizational excellence.

Notes

1. Collins and Porras, *Built to Last*.

2. Thomas J. Peters and Robert H. Waterman, *In Search of Excellence* (NY: Warner Business Books, 1982).

3. "Tom Peter's True Confessions," *Fast Company*, issue 53, December 2001, 78.

4. Christian Schwarz, *Natural Church Development* (Saint Charles, IL: Church Smart Resources, 1998).

5. Colossians 3:17.

6. Private conversation.

7. http://www.quality.nist.gov

About the Author

Gerald R. Chester, Ph.D. is the president of Strategies@Work, LLC, a privately held management consulting firm focused on helping organizations achieve excellent performance through the implementation of biblical philosophy, values, and principles.

During his career, Dr. Chester has gained extensive expertise in strategic planning, business development, financial management, and business operations. Since 1987, he has provided advisory services to more than seventy companies and organizations. His clients are owners, managers, and executives in a wide variety of businesses and organizations including manufacturing, distribution, technology, energy, retail, real estate development, construction, financial services, and communications. With rigorous technical training and practical business experience, Dr. Chester is well qualified to provide strategic thinking, coaching, and training.

Prior to beginning his consulting practice, Dr. Chester served as the president of his family's business. Under his leadership, the company's technical skills, image, and reputation were greatly enhanced as its annual revenue grew from $4 million to nearly $20 million.

Immediately after receiving his Ph.D. in physics from the University of Texas, Dr. Chester joined the research and development team of a Fortune 500 corporation. There he developed an ion gun for a proprietary ion implantation machine which increased semiconductor fabrication rates tenfold.

For Further Study

If you are interested in more information on the application of the Bible to organizational practices, please visit our Web site, www.strategieswork.com. The site includes audio files, newsletters, and other reference material that may be of interest to you.

To receive the free monthly newsletter from Strategies@Work, LLC, please sign up on the Web site.

Strategies@Work, LLC conducts seminars and other events concerning the application of a biblical worldview to individuals and organizations. To receive notices of these events, please sign up for the free monthly newsletter at the www.strategieswork.com. To book a seminar or an event, please communicate your request by e-mail to info@strategieswork.com.